"*Reaching Millennials* is a must-read for every pastor, lay minister, and church leader. David Stark has done a brilliant job of identifying what Millennials believe and what motivates them. If you want to welcome, celebrate, and engage Millennials in your church, then devour this book!"

—Mark Crea, CEO, Feed My Starving Children

"David Stark has written a penetrating and urgent analysis of a generation coming of age. This will be of interest to anyone concerned about the church and the future."

—John Ortberg, Senior Pastor, Menlo Church

"In *Reaching Millennials*, Stark conveys afresh the vital connection between the right mindset and an effective methodology as the church seeks to share the gospel with the Millennial generation. He encourages churches to have significant *reflective* conversations about mission prior to any *reactive* response, as one without the other seldom produces good fruit. Read and learn!"

—Rev. Mark R. Stromberg, Superintendent, Northwest Conference of the Evangelical Covenant Church

"For many years, David and I have grappled on how to connect with people outside the Christian faith. I was excited to see those thoughts in print. I would highly recommend this book to any Christian who wants to understand how to best connect with outsiders in today's cultural environment. I have experienced this at Habitat for Humanity, and am convinced that this approach is very effective in establishing the credibility to build spiritual friendships and invite people to consider church involvement."

—Jonathan Reckford, CEO, Habitat for Humanity

"Dave Stark gets Millennials. And this isn't easy. These young people are pragmatic idealists who are deeply committed to their networks, their friends, and to making a difference. But they distrust Christians and Christianity, so the task of the church and its leaders is more challenging than ever. Stark's book, using a pragmatic, realistic, and yes, a hopeful slate of ideas, will make a difference."

—James Wellman Jr., Professor and Chair, Comparative Religion Program, University of Washington–Seattle

REACHING
MILLENNIALS

Books by David Stark

FROM BETHANY HOUSE PUBLISHERS

LifeKeys and *LifeKeys Discovery Workbook*
(coauthored with Jane A. G. Kise and Sandra Krebs Hirsh)
Growing People Through Small Groups
Christ-Based Leadership
Reaching Millennials

REACHING
MILLENNIALS

PROVEN METHODS FOR ENGAGING
A YOUNGER GENERATION

DAVID STARK

BETHANYHOUSE

a division of Baker Publishing Group

Minneapolis, Minnesota

Published by Bethany House Publishers
11400 Hampshire Avenue South
Bloomington, Minnesota 55438
www.bethanyhouse.com

Bethany House Publishers is a division of
Baker Publishing Group, Grand Rapids, Michigan

Printed in the United States of America

ISBN 978-0-7642-1723-4

Library of Congress Control Number: 2016930528

Some names and identifying details have been changed to protect the privacy of those involved.

Cover design by Dan Pitts

16 17 18 19 20 21 22   7 6 5 4 3 2 1

To my sons, Dan and Kevin,
who were my first teachers about
the Millennial generation as they grew up.

To all the staff of Rustica Bakery in Minneapolis
who served me well as I wrote this book.

To all the great churches, coast to coast,
that are doing the work to represent Christ
to the younger generations.

Contents

Introduction

Just before I sat down to write this introduction, the Pew Research Center released its latest comprehensive survey of religious life in America. The findings, unfortunately, mirror what I have experienced on the ground consulting with churches over the past two decades. Increasingly, people are not going to church or affiliating with Christianity. The "unaffiliated" are growing quickly in numbers, while all branches of the Christian body in America are declining, with a few noted exceptions. But the part of the story I want to focus on is the younger generations, specifically Millennials, people born between 1978 and 1998. The report concludes:

> As the Millennial generation enters adulthood, its members display much lower levels of religious affiliation, including less connection with Christian churches, than older generations. Fully 36% of young Millennials (those between the ages of 18 and 24) are religiously unaffiliated, as are 34% of older Millennials (ages 25–33). And fewer than six-in-ten Millennials identify with any branch of Christianity, compared with seven-in-ten or more among older generations, including Baby Boomers and

Gen-Xers. Just 16% of Millennials are Catholic, and only 11% identify with mainline Protestantism. Roughly one-in-five are evangelical Protestants.[1]

I was talking about this challenge some years ago with leaders of a large African-American church in Memphis, Tennessee. It had all the vibrancy of a great church—three thousand people in worship, fabulous choirs and music, a talented senior pastor and associate pastors. The Civil Rights movement of the 1960s and 1970s freed up many to pursue higher education, and this church had attracted more PhDs, MDs, JDs, MBAs, and every other letter combination of professionals I had ever seen before. The problem was, the children and grandchildren were not in church nearly as often as their parents and grandparents.

As I was presenting information related to a strategic plan for the church, I mentioned that we were in a season where the cultural setting in America had gotten a lot tougher than it used to be. As is true in some African-American churches, audience participation is common. One woman in the back of the room shouted, "They're not coming, they're not coming." I appreciated her input. It was God's way of magnifying the reality we all face.

---•◉•---

It is vital today that we shift our focus and planning for this reality, not in resignation and defeat but by envisioning new ways to engage the culture and younger generations. This book is written to address how we do that, with many examples of thriving churches making this shift. The road ahead will not be easy, but God is moving to help us represent and re-present the gospel and Christianity to our skeptical, yet still spiritually hungry world.

This book is divided into two major sections. In the first part, "Mindset," I explore the understanding that Jesus and the apostles had toward engaging people outside of Christianity, whom I will call outsiders. I do not use the term *outsider* in a demeaning or degrading way. I simply use it to designate people who do not affiliate with Christianity. Returning to how Jesus and the apostles viewed and approached outsiders will challenge many Christians and confirm for others what they have already been thinking and feeling. But hopefully it will get us to think like the early church did in loving and reaching the world.

The second part of the book, Methodology, looks at how churches are shifting their strategy and tactics to enter back into relationship with people outside the church walls. Large parts of God's renewal of the Christian body are happening outside of a physical building with a sanctuary. But for the purpose of this book, I concentrate on churches that have a building or physical presence in their community. Still, many of the principles I share also apply to other expressions of Christian community.

Some readers will undoubtedly want to get to the methodology chapters quickly and skip the first half of the book. Use the book for your purposes, however it is useful. My one caution is this: Without the right mindset in your church, any methodology has a great chance of failure, so I ask that you keep *mindset* and *methodology* connected as a whole.

The good news is, God is very much at work today around us. Even so, it will help to keep the first part of the Serenity Prayer in mind: "God grant me the serenity to accept the things I cannot change; courage to change the things I can; and wisdom to know the difference." Again, this is far from surrender. It is a path to renewal. As Paul wrote,

> Now to him who is able to do immeasurably more than all we ask or imagine, according to his power that is at work within us, to him be glory in the church and in Christ Jesus throughout all generations, for ever and ever! Amen.
>
> Ephesians 3:20–21

PART ONE

MINDSET

CHAPTER 1

The Question Before the Questions

I spent many hours interviewing Millennials for this book. And with one group of women in their twenties, all good friends with very different spiritual and religious lives, I was looking forward to a particularly insightful, lively discussion.

My wife and I had invited them to our home for a dinner party. And the conversation early on was indeed energetic as they shared their opinions and stories about everyday life, technology, you name it. I eventually moved into a series of questions that were structured as word associations. I told them I wanted their honest impressions: good, bad, or otherwise.

All was great until I brought up the words *Jesus* and *Christianity*. Suddenly, the room went quiet—for a whole minute—until one young woman broke the ice and said, "Well, that silence speaks a lot."

Whether they were unwilling to talk because they knew they might offend their friends (not likely with this group), or they were simply afraid to express their true feelings, clearly both the Christians and outsiders in this group were uncomfortable about Jesus and Christianity.

Immediately I was reminded of David Kinnaman's work with Millennials, people whose age is broadly twenty to thirty-five today. Kinnaman has overseen many research projects on matters of faith, spirituality, and other topics for Barna Group. We'll be referring frequently to his bestselling book, *unChristian*, written with Gabe Lyons, but I want to focus initially on what he calls "the disastrous decade."

In 1996, 85 percent of young people had a *positive* impression of Christianity's role in society. By 2006, it had become dramatically worse.

> The image of the Christian faith has suffered a major setback. Our most recent data shows that young outsiders have lost much of their respect for the Christian faith. These days nearly two out of every five outsiders (38 percent) claim to have a "bad impression of present-day Christianity." Beyond this, one-third of young outsiders said that Christianity represents a negative image with which they would not want to be associated. Furthermore, one out of every six young outsiders (17 percent) indicates that he or she maintains "very bad" perceptions of the Christian faith. Though these hard-core critics represent only a minority of young outsiders, this group is at least three times larger than it was [in 1996].[1]

Most of these impressions came from firsthand experiences. "Eighty-five percent of young outsiders have had sufficient exposure to Christians and churches that they conclude present-day Christianity is hypocritical," Kinnaman says.[2]

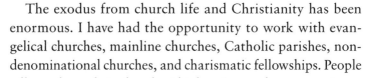

The exodus from church life and Christianity has been enormous. I have had the opportunity to work with evangelical churches, mainline churches, Catholic parishes, nondenominational churches, and charismatic fellowships. People tell me about their churches' high points and great moments, but in many cases they were decades ago, and since then they've seen declining attendance and engagement.

I was discussing these observations with a pastor who had a new intern from a local seminary spending a year with him as part of his education. In the middle of our conversation, he leaned over to his intern and said, "Welcome to the new reality: declining budgets and diminished expectations."

In many of the mainline denominations I interact with, leaders tell me that 80 percent or more of their churches are dying. In my research, some of this exodus stems from "internal" practices—how churches minister to people inside the church. But a greater factor is how the church interacts with outsiders and the polarizing rhetoric they often hear.

When I became a minister, I was excited to participate in the monthly gatherings of our presbytery, a regional group of ministers and lay leaders. At my first meeting, I was surprised to see quite a few people wearing a certain symbol, protesting the denomination's stance on what I will call "issue A." It was clear that if you weren't wearing the symbol, people assumed you were on the opposite side of the issue, whether true or not.

Each month it was surreal to see ministers and lay leaders divide into two long lines down the aisle of the host church sanctuary, waiting to get to the microphone to try to convince the audience of their point of view. It got so comical (tragic) that a colleague and I, a friend of mine who tended to be on the other side of many issues, began calling each other Pepsi and Coke. We knew we would cancel ourselves out when we voted, but we didn't allow it to destroy our relationship, making us the large exception to the rule. As issue after issue played out in the late 1990s, enormous amounts of time and money were spent on dealing with splits in the denomination, churches leaving, and hostile environments within presbyteries.

All this masked a much more important problem—the lack of thriving local churches, which was almost never discussed at the denomination level. The fallout has apparently spread. As I mentioned earlier, over 80 percent of the mainline churches are declining, and a good number may soon be gone completely.

Millennials, by the droves, are leaving the church. But there is an even more urgent and daunting result to all this fighting. Before we even approach young outsiders, they are loaded down by negative views toward Christians, churches, and Christianity.

I was teaching parts of this book at a local Christian university recently, and I brought my backpack with me. I gave each student a blank sheet of paper and asked them to write down the negative things their outside-the-church friends said about Christians. I then collected the papers and stuffed them into my backpack. We filled it easily.

Try this for yourself sometime. Put on a full backpack, walk around, and look at yourself in the mirror. Now imagine that over 40 percent of young people today are carrying around this backpack of negative impressions about Christianity before we even start building relationships with them and trying to discuss faith at all. The research shows that 57 percent of outsiders know evangelicals and 86 percent know a born-again Christian, whereas 49 percent have a bad impression of evangelical Christians, and 35 percent have a bad impression of born-again Christians.[3]

But enough on the negative side of this reality. I believe there is a way out of the past decades' counterproductive activity. It begins by thinking differently about our approach to ministry, especially when it comes to the younger generations. Jesus and the apostles had such a laser focus on the gospel that they made it the center of the work of the church. They viewed ministry and their mission to the world through the lens of what I call "the question before the questions."

The "Before" Question: How Do We Not Make It Hard for the Gentiles to Come to Faith?

This vital question comes directly from the first-century Council of Jerusalem: "It is my judgment, therefore, that we should not make it difficult for the Gentiles who are turning to God" (Acts 15:19). This statement, somewhat surprisingly made by James, came as the early church was struggling with questions of the law (which we will discuss in depth later). If you know the book of James even a little bit, he writes about how faith without works is dead. In fact, his letter seems to get close to saying it is not just the gospel that people need; it also must be played out in changes of behavior in people's lives. But even James saw the priority of placing the gospel over all things and how this should affect our approach to outsiders.

This conclusion did not come out of a vacuum. The apostles had heard the teaching of Jesus and seen his encounters with outsiders.

Some of my greatest memories with my wife and family have been dinner parties, life celebrations (anniversaries, birthdays, graduations, ordinations, etc.), and other joy-filled gatherings.

Several parables in the Bible not only involve celebrations and parties, but show the centrality of the gospel over all things. I want to focus on four parables in particular: the three "lost" parables in Luke 15 and the parable of the great banquet in Luke 14.

The parables of the lost sheep, the lost coin, and the lost son (prodigal son) are all set in the context of the Pharisees' criticism of Jesus for welcoming sinners and eating with them. It is important to notice initially that these three parables were meant to be a corrective to the Pharisees concerning how they approached people outside their church (the temple, in their case). Each of the three parables has a different setting but teaches a similar lesson:

1. There will be more rejoicing in heaven over one sinner who repents than ninety-nine righteous people who do not need repentance.
2. There is rejoicing in the presence of the angels over one sinner who repents.
3. The father tells his older son about the need to celebrate and be glad because his brother was dead but is alive again—was lost and now is found.

Whether people have wandered off (the lost sheep), have been misplaced (the lost coin), or deliberately walked away from God (the prodigal son), a great party is thrown in heaven when they are found and come back to God. This is what gives Jesus and the angels the greatest joy.

A fourth parable that mirrors this same priority of God's is the parable of the great banquet. God has invited people from all walks of life to celebrate together by throwing a banquet. God is also very upset when people don't attend the banquet for various reasons. So he invites every group possible to this banquet, because the desire of God is that the banquet be full. Wrapped in this parable is the passion of God that none would perish, but all would obtain eternal life.

This same focus is reflected in an encounter Jesus has with the disciples after they come back after ministering in the towns and countryside (Luke 10). The disciples are very excited about the power of the Holy Spirit to drive out demons and heal the sick. Jesus acknowledges that they have been given this authority over the demonic realm through the Holy Spirit, but what Jesus wants them to get excited about is that their name is written in the Book of Life because of the grace of God through faith.

When Jesus interacts with outsiders, he models the priority of the gospel. A vast majority of these encounters involve Jesus leading people to the living water, to be born again, to eat and never be hungry, and so on. Sin is mentioned only a few times in these encounters, and always to move the person toward repentance and to come back to God. A few examples:

1. Zacchaeus—I need to eat dinner with you tonight
2. Nicodemus—you need to be born again
3. Nathaniel—a man in whom there is no guile
4. Levi and the party—follow me
5. Peter—put down your nets in deep water
6. Man with leprosy—I am willing, be clean
7. Woman caught in adultery—neither do I condemn you
8. The paralytic lowered through the roof—your sins are forgiven
9. The woman at the well—if you asked him (Jesus) for a drink, he would have given you living water

All of this interaction and teaching by Jesus caused the apostles to view outsiders in a very specific way in order to keep the gospel central to their teachings and actions.

The Disciples Apply Jesus' Example

After Jesus spent forty days with the disciples and then ascended to heaven, the day of Pentecost began the public ministry of the apostles and other Christians to make disciples of all nations. It is my contention that to engage our culture, we must begin by changing our whole orientation toward outsiders, back to how Jesus and the apostles saw them, if we are to have a chance of influencing and/or recommending the Christian faith so they will genuinely consider following Christ in their lives. I know that God's action in the world is much bigger than our efforts, but I believe that the Holy Spirit is leading many pastors and lay leaders to reconsider how to participate with God in the work of the gospel and the kingdom in today's context. What I want to focus on in the book of Acts and a few other sections of the epistles are those passages in which the apostles are working out this "question before the questions": How can we not make it difficult for outsiders to come to faith?

Looking at the sum total of what was taught, decided, and modeled, we see that the apostles divided up God's revelation in relation to people outside the church (the way they approached the whole body of teaching and wisdom from the Scriptures) into five parts:

1. **Not God**—This area included parts of the surrounding culture that were counter to the teaching of the Bible. They did not try to embrace this part of the culture or acquiesce to the worldview that was clearly forbidden in Scripture.

2. **General revelation**—This is a category of beliefs and teachings that (the church believes) has been revealed by the Holy Spirit all over the world, regardless of background, belief system, or circumstance. The first example of this is the natural witness of creation mentioned in Romans 1, Psalm 33, and elsewhere. The second example is understandings of the world that agree with the worldview of Christians, even though the source of this wisdom comes from a source other than Scripture. One clear example is Paul's use of stoic philosophy in Acts 17 when talking to the Epicureans and Stoic philosophers on Mars Hill.

3. **Disputable matters in the church**—In Romans 14–15, Paul gives extensive teaching on how the church should handle disputable or nonessential matters in the church.

4. **The law**—This part of God's revelation includes all the commandments and teachings of how to follow God faithfully and live a Christian life.

5. **The gospel, Jesus, and the kingdom**—This essential part of God's revelation is best captured in the Apostles' Creed (even though parts of the creed are debated in some circles).

Understanding how the apostles used these five parts of God's revelation illustrates how central the "question before the questions" was to the early church. Over the next few chapters, we will look closely at each area to understand what it meant to the apostles and how it applies to the contemporary church today. A summary of this teaching is in the following chart, which will be presented again in the following chapters to help us see how everything fits together.

Category of Revelation	What Should We Focus On?	What Question Should We Ask?
Not God	Define yourself by what you're for and not by what you're against.	Will focusing on this idea or interest resonate with or discourage people who are considering Christianity?
General Revelation	Build bridges to ideas outside Christianity, and find as much common ground as possible.	Is this idea or area of knowledge consistent with biblical teaching on this topic?
Disputable Matters in the Church	Stick to the essentials of the faith and allow for diversity on anything else where Christians disagree.	Is this topic or area of interest a disputable or indisputable matter?
The Law	Limit the requirements to engage with the faith to the very small list (4) in Acts 15.	Are we making it hard for outsiders to come to the faith?
Gospel	Focus on thirsts, hurts, and journeys rather than what is wrong with the individual.	Are we using language and concepts that will be understood by our audience?

Please note that when I use the words *God's revelation*, I am speaking of the Scriptures. The five major categories are biblical categories that the apostles used (Gospel, The Law, and Disputable Matters in the Church) as well as two categories that are inferred by the actions of Jesus and the apostles (General Revelation and Not God).

Overall, in the first part of this book, I want to communicate:

1. First, the apostles and Jesus had a worldview and mindset that viewed all of Scriptures and the revelation of God through the five categories summarized in the chart.

2. These categories filtered how they went about using the revelation of God with outsiders and insiders, whom they treated very differently as they approached evangelism. Again, I use the term *outsiders* for those people who do not yet believe the claims of Christianity and *insiders* for those who are followers of Jesus and the kingdom.

3. We, in turn, need to heed the wisdom and pattern that the apostles and Jesus had in understanding ministry and mission to those outside the faith in order to genuinely represent Christianity, however imperfectly, to a world that is skeptical, neutral, and negative toward the Christian faith.

4. In each category in the chart, I have framed a question that the apostles asked or used as a filter when they were engaging decisions of how best to communicate the good news to a variety of audiences in the Roman Empire.

5. These questions directed what would be emphasized, modified, or left out completely as they interacted with those outside the faith, either by way of direct encounter or by instructions they gave to the churches to "make the most of every opportunity" (Colossians 4:5).

6. Much of the unnecessary (in my opinion) devastation of reputation and engagement that happened throughout

the latter part of the twentieth century in churches in America stemmed from ignoring these patterns and the wisdom of the apostles and Jesus.

7. Part of the renewal of the church in America and restoration of reputation, as well as witness and proclamation by Christians, begins by re-embracing this orientation to those outside the church. I have mentioned in each category in the chart one question the apostles asked about each part of God's revelation, and one focus or insight that summarizes how we are to approach this category of God's revelation with outsiders.

You'll see that in the following five chapters I share a representative text from Jesus or the apostles' experience that illustrates their interactions with various subcultures. (The biblical texts I have chosen are only one of a series of texts that could be quoted, which is why I consider them representative.) After gleaning principles from each biblical passage, I will then talk about how churches and church leaders are applying this to their communities today.

My biggest concern is that I have met only a few Christian leaders who start their understanding of missional activity and evangelistic strategy by asking how not to make it hard for the Gentiles (people outside the faith) to come to faith in Christ. The way is already narrow, as Jesus teaches in the Gospels. We should not make it narrower by overlooking or misunderstanding the apostles' faithful witness to the world.

Category of Revelation	What Should We Focus On?	What Question Should We Ask?
Not God	Define yourself by what you're for and not by what you're against.	Will focusing on this idea or interest resonate with or discourage people who are considering Christianity?
General Revelation	Build bridges to ideas outside Christianity, and find as much common ground as possible.	Is this idea or area of knowledge consistent with biblical teaching on this topic?
Disputable Matters in the Church	Stick to the essentials of the faith and allow for diversity on anything else where Christians disagree.	Is this topic or area of interest a disputable or indisputable matter?
The Law	Limit the requirements to engage with the faith to the very small list (4) in Acts 15.	Are we making it hard for outsiders to come to the faith?
Gospel	Focus on thirsts, hurts, and journeys rather than what is wrong with the individual.	Are we using language and concepts that will be understood by our audience?

CHAPTER 2

Handling Cultural Issues We Know Are "Not God"

Now Jesus learned that the Pharisees had heard that he was gaining and baptizing more disciples than John—although in fact it was not Jesus who baptized, but his disciples. So he left Judea and went back once more to Galilee.

Now he had to go through Samaria. So he came to a town in Samaria called Sychar, near the plot of ground Jacob had given to his son Joseph. Jacob's well was there, and Jesus, tired as he was from the journey, sat down by the well. It was about noon.

When a Samaritan woman came to draw water, Jesus said to her, "Will you give me a drink?" (His disciples had gone into the town to buy food.)

The Samaritan woman said to him, "You are a Jew and I am a Samaritan woman. How can you ask me for a drink?" (For Jews do not associate with Samaritans.)

Jesus answered her, "If you knew the gift of God and who it is that asks you for a drink, you would have asked him and he would have given you living water."

"Sir," the woman said, "you have nothing to draw with and the well is deep. Where can you get this living water? Are you greater than our father Jacob, who gave us the well and drank from it himself, as did also his sons and his livestock?"

Jesus answered, "Everyone who drinks this water will be thirsty again, but whoever drinks the water I give them will never thirst. Indeed, the water I give them will become in them a spring of water welling up to eternal life.

The woman said to him, "Sir, give me this water so that I won't get thirsty and have to keep coming here to draw water."

John 4:1–15

On a trip to San Francisco, I had the opportunity to have lunch with the young leaders at a church known for its impactful ministry to college students from a campus nearby. We talked that day about many aspects of students' lives, but I was captured by one response to a question I had about social media. The leader of the group commented that she did not use Facebook much anymore because "I can't keep my profile interesting and my body thin enough to post pictures."

Keep in mind, this is the generation whose parents unconditionally cheered them on, insisting they could accomplish anything and everything, always building up their self-worth and encouraging a strong self-identity. Then came the technology that defined this generation—Facebook. These days, communication with a wide assortment of friends is constant, and outward-focused activity is the norm as people share their lives with their virtual tribes.

Speaking as a baby boomer, I find these new technologies exciting to use because now I do not have to write so many letters or make so many phone calls to keep people updated on my life. But for all the great positives about technology and social media, it can pressure people to have exciting adventures and take wonderful pictures to post on their Facebook wall. Suddenly, pretty much everyone has a public image. At the same time, we've all had to become critics, attuned to differentiating what is real and what is hype.

Thanks in part to all the new media channels, Millennials, in particular, have been bombarded with marketing messages. For as long as they can remember, they've heard promises for this and claims for that. Therefore, they are hypersensitive and highly sensitive to what people say they believe, promote, or do, and the observable true reality about a person, product, or organization.

This sensibility seems to extend to the TV-watching preferences of young people. One woman told me, "Have you ever noticed that in scripted TV shows, people always have the right words to say, have the right background music, wear cutting-edge clothes and have beautiful bodies, and any problem can be wrapped up in one or two segments? Get real. Reality TV has some scripting and editing, but it's much closer to authentic, everyday people doing exciting things or trying to excel at something."

All of this means that outsiders today evaluate Christianity and get a sense of who we are not by our words but by how we live and act. Young outsiders are pushed away by inauthenticity and hypocrisy. They don't expect someone to live a "perfect" life, because they already frame moral decisions as mostly gray in a complex, contextual, and very diverse world. But what pushes them away is when a person or group claims to be one thing but acts like something else. To mention Kinnaman's work again— 84 percent of the outsiders know a Christian personally, but only 15 percent see our lives as different from non-Christians.[1]

Why is this? Unfortunately, the perception of outsiders is close to reality. Research by Barna Group and others has shown there is little difference in the moral attitudes and behaviors of people inside and outside the church. Still, the problem is deeper than a sense of hypocrisy.

Let's step back a minute and discuss how we end up sending the impression of moral superiority in the first place. It usually starts with good intentions, sparked by a strong desire to follow Jesus. We read the Bible, learn as much as we can from pastors and other leaders, and do our best to grow in faith and avoid sin. Unfortunately, many Christians—often older ones—believe the *most* important part of following Jesus is to avoid sin rather than, say, bear fruit (love, joy, peace, etc.), love their neighbors, or seek God's will. Their focus is on becoming morally better. As a consequence, they wrongly think outsiders will not follow Jesus because they cannot or will not change their moral lives.

Not Just Being "Against Something"

A well-known song takes its message from the Bible: People should know we are Christians by our love (John 13:35). But when outsiders observe Christians carrying themselves with an air of moral superiority, and then they observe we're flawed just like them, they see it as hypocrisy. Philip Yancey, in his book *Vanishing Grace*, puts it this way:

> I once conducted an informal survey among airline seatmates and other strangers willing to strike up a conversation. When I say the word "evangelical," what comes to mind? In response I would usually hear the word "against": evangelicals are against abortion, against pornography, against gay rights, against universal health care, against evolution, against immigration. Outsiders regard evangelicals as moralists who want to impose their "head" beliefs on a diverse society. As [theologian] Miroslav Volf noted, when a religion, any religion, tries to force itself on others who do not share their belief, it creates a backlash and stirs up opposition.[2]

I saw this come through in my interviews in several ways. I was working on this book in a park one day when I struck up a conversation with a group of young people celebrating a birthday. They asked what I was working on, which opened the door to my asking about their experiences with Christians. One woman said she had attended a Bible study because she was curious about Jesus, but she quickly learned that the Christians there did not respect or accept her because of some aspect of her lifestyle. She left the group, saying she couldn't hear anything about Jesus because the nonverbal rejection was so loud it muffled other voices. Another person told me about feeling like she didn't "measure up" when she asked Christians questions or shared viewpoints that were not "acceptable."

One story will help drive this point home. There was a time when my wife and I were close friends with a family that included two adult brothers. One brother attended the church where I was a pastor, and the other was part of a couple we were good friends with in our neighborhood. The man in our church prayed for and tried to witness to his brother. The problem was, the "witness" he was trying to portray was how faith made the lives of his family better than his brother's family. One day when we were all together for dinner, the Christian brother blurted out, "How come you haven't become a Christian? Haven't I convinced you of the superiority of this way of life?"

This, of course, was not well-received for multiple reasons. For starters, both brothers had major problems with alcohol in their lives, yet the "outsider" brother was the one who had gone through AA and been sober for years. Also, for years, the couple who attended our church had communicated to the brother's family in not-so-subtle ways how their kids were better athletes, scholars, and generally more successful people. The witness he thought he should be giving was one of superior living rather than the love of God for all people.

Interactions like these create the impression that Christians are "the against people," judging others for perceived moral inferiority. As indicated before, Jesus did not take the pathway of judgment with outsiders, but instead he led with love, acceptance, and forgiveness.

Look at the Bible story that led off this chapter and notice how Jesus treated the Samaritan woman—someone with well-fortified walls against the faith (which is the condition of most of the younger generations in America today).

Back then, there was widespread hatred and demeaning attitudes between the Samaritans and Jews. Things had gotten so bad that it was considered defiling or unclean to even pass through Samaritan territory. Talk about moral superiority on steroids. But Jesus refuses to follow this approach with outsiders, or women, or even a "sinful woman," for that matter. He starts by being vulnerable about needing water, which would become the center of their conversation. The woman immediately brings up the hurtful box that she has been put in by the judgment and rejection of the Jews, saying, "You are a Jew, and I am a Samaritan, how can you ask me for a drink?"

This is exactly what will happen for many of us as we approach a culture that has experienced judgment and rejection from Christians. The barriers and baggage that people have are real, and until they are expressed, many people will not go further. Jesus, in response, does not try to justify, explain away, or correct the Samaritan woman's doctrine at all. He does not want to sidetrack the conversation about water, which is where the Good News of the gospel will be revealed. This first principle is so important for interacting with outsiders today.

When people express hurts, barriers, or experiences that seem like roadblocks to interacting with Christians in the first place, don't take the bait and discuss morality or in any way justify the poor behavior they have experienced. In fact, letting people get their pain out is many times a precursor for them to talk further.

In the Bible story, Jesus stays on topic about living water, but a second potential barrier in their conversation arises. The Samaritan woman interprets literally what Jesus means spiritually—that actual water will well up inside of her. This illustrates another important principle: For many outsiders today, common Christian words sound like a foreign language (e.g., *sanctification*, the *Trinity*, *born again*). From the Bible stories we tell to discussing theological issues, we need to use everyday language. And communication is a two-way street, of course. Understanding the outsider's vocabulary has been part of the DNA of many successful churches, usually by the senior leadership researching the community around them and getting to know the so-called Saddleback Sams and Unchurched Harrys (more on this in the next chapter).

Jesus clarifies to the Samaritan exactly what he means about this water, which is that it's spiritually inside a person, it will result in eternal life, and it's a spring that will enable her to never thirst again. But he knows there are still other barriers to the woman following him, so he asks her to call her husband. She speaks honestly about her situation: She has no husband.

At this point the Holy Spirit speaks to Jesus what is called a "word of knowledge" in spiritual-gift circles, meaning he knows facts about her situation that he could not have known unless they were revealed to him. Even in bringing up her adulterous behavior, his purpose is to affirm her honesty and to begin to give her evidence that he is much more than a man. She responds by telling him that she now knows he is a prophet sent by God.

Then the woman brings up another barrier that prevents her from considering Jesus' claims. She mentions a belief the Jews have that contradicts the Samaritans' own practice of spiritual expression. But notice what Jesus does with this question. He says the issue of worship is something much deeper than mountains and temples, and he even points out that in this part of Jewish and Samaritan practice, things are going to change for both of them. In other words, he gets at the core of the issue, which is that it's not as important where you worship as it is that you do so in Spirit and truth.

Many Millennials disagree with what Christians claim to believe about worship, having had their own experiences of spiritual practice. Jesus was willing to say the issue is more complicated than how it is being framed both by Jewish people and Samaritan people.

In today's context—in which we Google everything—everyone can surf the Internet and hear multiple points of views on anything they want. When outsiders ask us tough questions and we frame our answers as "either/or" (*either* this is right *or* that is right, but not both), they consider it intellectually insulting. They reject simple answers, and they want us to grapple with the complexity of issues.

A few experiences have helped me understand what this "either/or" approach sounds like to younger generations. Tolerance is highly valued by young people, making it difficult for them to agree that something is true in all circumstances, everywhere, regardless of nation, religious background, context, or the particular day or year we find ourselves in.

One year on a college tour with one of my sons, the school he was considering split the parents into a separate group from the potential students. We parents had the opportunity to hear a lecture that happened to be about the philosophical grounding of the United States. I love learning, especially about philosophy, so I listened to the professor with a keen ear. At the end was a question and answer period, so I asked him what, if anything, had changed during his teaching career. Without missing a beat, he said that twenty years ago, when he asked students to write about something they believed to be true and then defend it philosophically, they easily tackled the assignment. Today's students, he said, struggle to identify just one thing they believe is true.

I saw this in action as I was talking with a Millennial pastor about this book. He said, "When you engage these kinds of questions with anyone in this generation, in my experience, they are not, at first, focused primarily on debating the right or wrong of their position or yours. They are focused on the absurdity in this massively diverse world that Christians are not even acknowledging that there are other points of view on the issue, and the complexity of the issue when it is applied in vastly different cultural environments."

Returning to the Samaritan woman's question about worship practices, rather than getting stuck in a simplistic discussion about whether worship requires a mountain or a temple, Jesus says it really concerns the heart and Spirit of God. His answer removes the barrier for her, and from there Jesus gets to the whole point of this encounter and introduces the woman to the Messiah, himself. By way of summary, Jesus always keeps the final destination in his line of sight, which is the gospel and the realty of who he is.

I cannot say it forcefully enough: KEEP THE MAIN THING, THE MAIN THING (to put it in Stephen Covey language). For Christians, the Good News of Jesus Christ as Savior and Lord will always be the main thing! Sadly, much of the church does not keep this the center of what their church is about, and this misstep is picked up by the attuned radar of younger generations.

We need to assume that barriers already exist to Christians and Christianity in every outsider we meet. These barriers are based on real experiences with churches and Christians. These generations, for the most part, will not give us time to get our act together or give us the benefit of the doubt. If we do not change how we approach them—focusing our conversation on the Good News of grace instead of on correcting their philosophical perspective or trying to change their doctrine or morality—the conversation will be over very quickly. Imagine just how long the conversation would have lasted if Jesus had engaged the woman at the well with her wrong doctrine, moral failure, or bigotry toward Jews. Probably a few seconds at best.

When we encounter outsiders who are clearly doing something we disagree with, or have strong barriers to Christianity built up by bad experiences, the question we should ask ourselves is this: Is my focus on the Good News that Christianity offers, or is it on trying to change something about their morality or their lifestyle, or on justifying the bad experiences they have had with Christians or churches in their past?

Along with this question, I want to give you one way to think about how you are doing in changing your focus. Paul told us in 2 Corinthians that we are the aroma of Christ, so I am going to call this the smell test (because, as Paul says, we Christians already smell sour to those who are outsiders). We should not "smell" like the Pharisee in the parable of the Pharisee and the Publican, who carries himself with a sense of superiority. He thinks, *God, I thank you that I am not like other people—robbers, evildoers, adulterers, even that tax collector.* In other words, "I am avoiding a few big sins, and therefore my standing with God is higher than those 'other people.'"

Instead, our aroma should be like the tax collector, who cannot even look up at heaven, and beats his chest in frustration and disappointment with himself as he says, "God, have mercy on me, a sinner." Most of the time when we approach people by being real about our own struggles, grateful that God has loved us and forgiven us of our sin, this will take down the walls or barriers with others rather than making the walls even higher.

In conclusion, we need to stay focused on the Good News of God's grace, not on the things we object to in the lives of outsiders. Paraphrasing what pastor and author John Ortberg has said frequently in his speaking and teaching, organizations and spiritual movements that are growing and expanding are focused on the center, describing what they are *for*. Organizations and movements that are decaying or declining are focused on the boundaries, or what they are *against*.

Category of Revelation	What Should We Focus On?	What Question Should We Ask?
Not God	Define yourself by what you're for and not by what you're against.	Will focusing on this idea or interest resonate with or discourage people who are considering Christianity?
General Revelation	Build bridges to ideas outside Christianity, and find as much common ground as possible.	Is this idea or area of knowledge consistent with biblical teaching on this topic?
Disputable Matters in the Church	Stick to the essentials of the faith and allow for diversity on anything else where Christians disagree.	Is this topic or area of interest a disputable or indisputable matter?
The Law	Limit the requirements to engage with the faith to the very small list (4) in Acts 15.	Are we making it hard for outsiders to come to the faith?
Gospel	Focus on thirsts, hurts, and journeys rather than what is wrong with the individual.	Are we using language and concepts that will be understood by our audience?

CHAPTER 3

General Revelation—Finding Community and Common Ground

Though I am free and belong to no one, I have made myself a slave to everyone, to win as many as possible. To the Jews I became like a Jew, to win the Jews. To those under the law I became like one under the law (though I myself am not under the law), so as to win those under the law. To those not having the law I became like one not having the law (though I am not free from God's law but am under Christ's law), so as to win those not having the law. To the weak I became weak, to win the weak. I have become all things to all people so that by all possible means I might save some. I do all this for the sake of the gospel, that I may share in its blessings.

1 Corinthians 9:19–23

While Paul was waiting for them in Athens, he was greatly distressed to see that the city was full of idols. So he reasoned in the synagogue with the Jews and the God-fearing Greeks, as well as in the marketplace day by day with those who happened to be there. A group of Epicurean and Stoic philosophers began to dispute with him. Some of them asked, "What is this babbler trying to say?" Others remarked, "He seems to be advocating foreign gods." They said this because Paul was preaching the good news about Jesus and the resurrection. Then they took him and brought him to a meeting of the Areopagus, where they said to him, "May we know what this new teaching is that you are presenting? You are bringing some strange ideas to our ears, and we want to know what they mean." (All the Athenians and the foreigners who lived there spent their time doing nothing but talking about and listening to the latest ideas.)

Paul then stood up in the meeting of the Areopagus and said: "Men of Athens! I see that in every way you are very religious.

For as I walked around and looked carefully at your objects of worship, I even found an altar with this inscription: to an unknown god. Now what you worship as something unknown I am going to proclaim to you.

"The God who made the world and everything in it is the Lord of heaven and earth and does not live in temples built by hands. And he is not served by human hands, as if he needed anything, because he himself gives all men life and breath and everything else. From one man he made every nation of men, that they should inhabit the whole earth; and he determined the times set for them and the exact places where they should live. God did this so that men would seek him and perhaps reach out for him and find him, though he is not far from each one of us. 'For in him we live and move and have our being.' As some of your own poets have said, 'We are his offspring.'

"Therefore since we are God's offspring, we should not think that the divine being is like gold or silver or stone—an image made by man's design and skill. In the past God overlooked such ignorance, but now he commands all people everywhere to repent. For he has set a day when he will judge the world with justice by the man he has appointed. He has given proof of this to all men by raising him from the dead."

When they heard about the resurrection of the dead, some of them sneered, but others said, "We want to hear you again on this subject." At that, Paul left the Council. A few men became followers of Paul and believed. Among them was Dionysius, a member of the Areopagus, also a woman named Damaris, and a number of others.

Acts 17:16–34

In addition to being a church consultant, I also work with businesses. In this capacity, I recently attended a conference in New York City that I was excited about because the people there were working on the same ideas I have been pursuing for years. The main speaker, a management consultant known internationally, is a professed Christian. My alma mater is Princeton Seminary, so I stayed outside the city and took the train to Grand Central Station, and then walked the few blocks to the conference. The speakers on the schedule had come from all over the world.

Gathered with a hundred-plus like-minded people, I could not wait to digest the speakers' ideas and strike up conversations during the breaks. But I got a big shock. As I walked around the lobby, everyone was on their cell phones, laptops, or iPads, undoubtedly responding to emails, tweets, texts, Facebook posts, and so on. There we were, in an eerie silence, having driven or flown from all over to be together, yet each of us was alone. It did not help that the structure of the conference didn't include small groups, but it seemed to me we could have easily facilitated conversations. The Millennial-aged hostess, acknowledging the lack of interaction in the conference, tried to get us to text, tweet, or communicate in some other way, but to no avail.

Sherry Turkle, in her book *Alone Together*, describes a similar experience:

I have often observed this distinctive confusion: these days, whether you are online or not, it is easy for people to end up

44

unsure if they are closer together or further apart. I remember my own sense of disorientation the first time I realized that I was "alone together." I had traveled an exhausting thirty-six hours to attend a conference on advanced robotic technology held in central Japan. The packed grand ballroom was WiFi enabled: the speaker was using the Web for his presentation, laptops were open throughout the audience, and fingers were flying, and there was a sense of great concentration and intensity. But not many were attending to the speaker. Most people seemed to be doing their email, downloading files, and surfing the Net. . . .

Outside, in the hallways, the people around me were looking past me to virtual others. They were on their laptops and cellphones, connecting to colleagues at the conference around them and to others around the globe. There, but not there. . . . At this conference it was clear that what people mostly want from public space is a chance to be with their personal networks.[1]

Why are we seeing this "alone together" reality? Part of the story is how America has sorted itself into specific groups (you could call them cohorts, tribes, lifestyle segments, etc.). American religion and spirituality have followed the same path. In *The Big Sort*, author Bill Bishop argues that because of our mobility as a nation, and also our ability to choose where we live, we have consciously and unconsciously chosen to live near people with whom we have many cultural aspects in common. He outlines this in detailed ways in his book, but for our purposes, the important trend is that the more diverse America becomes, the more homogeneous it becomes.

No, that's not a misprint. Bishop argues that people, quite recently, have rearranged themselves into discrete enclaves that have little to say to one another and little incentive to bother trying. "As Americans have moved over the past three decades," the author proclaims, "they have clustered in communities of sameness, among people with similar ways of life, beliefs, and, in the end, politics."[2]

Bishop's observations started formulating when he realized his Austin, Texas, neighborhood included virtually no Republicans. In another community of similar size nearby, there were very few Democrats. Thirty years earlier, that uniformity would not have been possible, he argued. Back then, values, ideologies, and partisanship would have mingled in even the most compact neighborhoods, wards, or districts.

I have always been skeptical about the clustering thesis myself, but there is one simple statistic, rightly seized on by Bishop, that is difficult to explain away: "In 1976, less than a quarter of the American people lived in so-called landslide counties—that is, counties in which the spread between the two major presidential candidates was 20 percentage points or more. By 2004, nearly half of us lived in this kind of politically tilted territory."[3] This has huge implications for the church as we try to engage the communities around us, because we will find they are finely sorted in terms of values, beliefs, and ideologies—especially among younger generations.

We need to be aware that another layer of sorting is happening in our communities. According to a Pew Research Center report,

> People still value neighbors, because living nearby remains important for everyday socializing and for dealing with emergencies, large and small. Yet, neighbors are only about 10% of people's significant ties. As a result, people's social routines are different from those of their parents and their grandparents. Although people see their coworkers and neighbors often, most of their important contacts are with people who live elsewhere in the city, region, nation, and abroad. The internet, either mobile or wired, is especially valuable for those kinds of connections.[4]

In other words, people go farther and create their own Internets by the various connections they set up: "Networked technology has also changed the social point of contact from the household (and workgroup) to the individual. Each person also creates their own Internet, tailored to her needs. Each person builds and maintains their own network, and maintains it through their own address book, and individually controlled emails, screen names, social technological filters, and mobile phone numbers."[5] Consequently, the world of many young people is primarily the social world they build online, augmented by face-to-face meetings.

Communities in Action

How does all this concern Millennials and faith involvement? One important insight comes from understanding how these younger generations filter options and ideas amongst the bombardment of messages that ask for their time and engagement. The most important decision-making factor is the opinions and perspectives of their networks—whether that includes Christians and churches or not—with whom they will share their experiences.

Once again, the Pew Research Center provides a helpful clarification:

> In an environment of information overabundance, social networks have become a tool that helps people figure out how to drink from the proverbial fire hose. A mantra for many is: "If news is important, it will find its way to me." For Millennials, this is a primary reason to check their social networking spaces with some regularity. Half of Millennial users of social networking sites check them multiple times a day, compared with less than a third of the Baby boomers who do so. In addition, people often turn to their social networks to help them evaluate the new information they encounter. For example, Millennials are the most likely generation to use online social spaces to discuss and share health information and need to make health decisions. Also, about 3 in 10 social networking Millennials say they have gotten more involved in a political cause after discussing it or

reading about it in social networking spaces. . . . Millennials are also twice as likely as Boomers to say they have become less active in a cause after reading what their friends said about it on social networking sites.[6]

"We are a feedback generation," one woman told me in an interview. Her comment reminded me of a conversation I had with a soon-to-be-bride who was in her midtwenties and wanted me to officiate the wedding. As we began to talk, she was clearly upset, and I asked what was wrong. It had only been a week since her engagement, and she had just shared the news with her network of girlfriends. Sadly, their initial feedback was negative. As I inquired further, she talked about the pressure to not only find the right man to marry, but he had to be someone who would win her girlfriends' approval. In his book *Urban Tribes*, Ethan Watters came to the conclusion that people are delaying marriage because they have such a strong network of friends who help them with support and advice about many things in their lives—this also includes who they marry.

On the other hand, this "feedback generation" also influences one another to do great things. Recently, I asked one of my sons if he wanted to work on a Feed My Starving Children event I was leading at a local church. Feed My Starving Children is a nonprofit organization that uses volunteers to pack dry meals to be sent to the most distressed parts of the world. My son said yes, and then told his network about it. We ended up taking eight or so of his friends, most of whom had not been in a church in years. (I will share more about these community events later.)

To summarize what I am saying so far, society is very segmented right now, not only in neighborhoods but also in online networks where important decisions are processed with others. What makes this somewhat disconcerting is that Christians have also created a subculture unto themselves.

Unfortunately, this has led many to conclude that Christians are "out of touch, out of tune, uninformed, and clueless about life outside the bubble."[7] One self-aware Christian woman put it this way to David Kinnaman:

> So many Christians are caught up in the Christian subculture and are completely closed off from the world. We go to church on Wednesdays, Sundays, and sometimes on Saturdays. We attend a small group on Tuesday night and serve on various committees and boards. We go to barbeques with our Christian friends and plan group outings. We are closed off from the world. Even if we wanted to reach out to non-Christians, we don't have the time and we don't know how. The only way we know how to reach out is to invite people into our Christian social circle.[8]

This cloistering is especially damaging when it comes to religion and spirituality. To understand this, I need to give a little background. Robert Wuthnow, a very insightful Princeton sociologist, wrote a book called *After Faith*, in which he detailed the exit of the baby boomer generation from the church.

It is a nuanced argument, but one of the most important changes that happened in the American culture during the 1970s and 1980s was the split of religion from the world of spirituality. Spirituality, for those outside the church, became defined as "Making meaning and finding purpose by integrating experiences from a multiple set of sources and inputs." Religion became relegated to one option among many possible bases for your spirituality. Consequently, since that time, people outside the church have been weaving a tapestry of inputs (yoga retreats, massage therapists, giving back through charitable organizations, treks and journeys in nature) to define their spiritual life.

In my interviews with Millennials, spirituality is clearly popular, but it is a very individual journey. A recent movie entitled *Wild* tells the story of one young woman walking the Pacific Crest Trail after disasters happen in her marriage, family, and life. The movie does a good job illustrating this sense of spiritual quest. The woman is journeying alone, although various people are helpful as guides along the way. A red fox becomes her spiritual fellow traveler that leaves once she makes her journey. She goes through many emotional crises, including hating God for not saving her mom when she prayed at one time in her life. She ends up working it all through at the Bridge of the Gods, a park in northern Oregon. For young people, this type of spiritual journey is both vital and mysterious. Religion, on the other hand, can be seen as dull and lifeless.

I was talking with a woman after a business conference we attended, and I told her about the book I was working on. She said her father (probably about my age) is always trying to get her to go back to church anytime she struggles with something. She said that three songs and a "twenty-minute monologue" is not at all motivating to her. That opinion, by the way, is shared by about 70 percent of the younger generation, according to Barna Group.[9]

Where Do We Go From Here?

So how do we respond to these realities? First, let's start with the call of Jesus for us to be salt and light in the world. We are not to be cloistered; we should live our lives for everyone to see. Second, Paul tells us in 1 Corinthians 9 to become like the Romans to win the Romans, the Greeks to win the Greeks. In other words, the apostles and Jesus contextualized their ministries according to the culture they found themselves embedded in. Rather than creating their own subculture, the apostles tried to understand and engage other cultures.

Many successful churches in America started with this fundamental premise. In the early days of Saddleback Church in Southern California, pastor Rick Warren walked the nearby neighborhoods and talked with people until he could understand "Saddleback Sam," an aggregate description of the normal life of people outside the church around him. And in Chicago, Bill Hybels, pastor of Willow Creek Community Church, did something similar and came up with "Unchurched Harry," which he gleaned from his experiences with people outside the church. He knew he could not invite outsiders to his church the way it was. Both became huge churches for many reasons, not the least of which was following Paul's model and becoming like the outsiders to win the outsiders.

Let's look closely at Paul's approach in Acts 17 while he was waiting for Silas and Timothy. Many things happen in this text, but I want to focus on the concept of general revelation. In theology, general revelation refers to an understanding of God and spiritual matters that is plainly available to all people—discovered through natural means such as observations of nature (the physical universe), philosophy and reasoning, human conscience, or a providential view of history. The underlying belief is that people everywhere have some knowledge of God available to them, even if they do not acknowledge him, or they view him in a different way from Christianity.

In the time of Paul, most citizens of Athens were polytheists who built altars to hundreds of gods. The altar to the unknown god had come about years earlier during a plague. Since altars and sacrifices to the "known" gods had not brought relief, someone had the idea to build an altar to the unknown god, and the plague began to decrease in Athens.

Within the city there were a couple of philosophical schools that did not agree with the norm of polytheism, namely the Epicureans and Stoic philosophers. Paul, who grew up in Tarsus, had been exposed through his educational background to the Scriptures and philosophies of the Stoics and Epicureans and would know them well. He therefore uses the altar of the unknown god to begin his outdoor preaching in the large marketplace in Athens called the Agora. As he stated in his sermon on Mars Hill, this was very common in Athens at this time, and would not seem weird or out of place because the Athenians liked debating philosophical and religious ideas in the open air of the Agora. Paul decided to focus his remarks on the Stoics and Epicureans because he could speak in their language and knew their cultural and spiritual backgrounds. He then chose what I call a "beachhead" in the culture that was widely accepted, the altar to the unknown God, as a starting point for his remarks. Let's look again at the text of Mars Hill in Acts 17:

> Paul then stood up in the meeting of the Areopagus and said: "People of Athens! I see that in every way you are very religious. For as I walked around and looked carefully at your objects of worship, I even found an altar with this inscription: to an unknown god. So you are ignorant of the very thing you worship—and this is what I am going to proclaim to you.
>
> "The God who made the world and everything in it is the Lord of heaven and earth and does not live in temples built by human hands. And he is not served by human hands, as if he needed anything. Rather, he himself gives everyone life and breath and everything else. From one man he made all the nations, that they should inhabit the whole earth; and he marked out their appointed times in history and the boundaries of their lands. God did this so that they would seek him and perhaps reach out for him and find him, though he is not far from any one of us. 'For in him we live and move and have our being.' As some of your own poets have said, 'We are his offspring.'
>
> "Therefore since we are God's offspring, we should not think that the divine being is like gold or silver or stone—an image made by human design and skill. In the past God overlooked such ignorance, but now he commands all people everywhere to repent. For he has set a day when he will judge the world

with justice by the man he has appointed. He has given proof of this to everyone by raising him from the dead."

When they heard about the resurrection of the dead, some of them sneered, but others said, "We want to hear you again on this subject." At that, Paul left the Council. Some of the people became followers of Paul and believed. Among them was Dionysius, a member of the Areopagus, also a woman named Damaris, and a number of others.

Acts 17:22–34

Notice that Paul does not begin his address as a prophet would, condemning their idolatry, but rather as an evangelist. He sees through their idol worship to their motivation underneath, which is to seek God. Understanding his audience, he starts off by talking about things the Epicureans and Stoics agreed on. He also quotes their holy Scriptures twice, which is the poetry mentioned. Paul then goes on to talk about the personal God and the resurrection from the dead, which some would not have any part of, he says, but "some . . . believed."

There are a few important principles drawn from this text that apply to the whole area of general revelation.

1. Paul is looking for common ground with the Athenians as a starting point of the interaction. Because of general revelation, believers and outsiders of many stripes hold certain values, beliefs, and convictions in common. And to reach the younger generations around us, common ground is plentiful and effective. In his book *Vanishing Grace*, Philip Yancey observes:

> Dag Hammerskjöld, who served as secretary-general of the United Nations during some of the tensest days of the Cold War, explained that in dealing with adversaries he would begin by searching for the smallest point of common ground. When he found a single point of agreement

between two parties, he then worked toward building relationship and trust that could perhaps lead to honest dialogue on harder issues. As a model, he looked to Jesus, who was God's way of sharing the common ground of humanity: "He sat at meals with publicans and sinners, he consorted with harlots."

Communicating faith to skeptics and outsiders usually works best when it emphasizes how we are alike, not how we are different. I am learning to resist the tendency to see others as opponents or targets and instead look for areas of common ground, places where we can stand together.[10]

2. Paul saw beyond the surface and built a bridge to the spirituality of his listeners. We miss completely that many people outside the church want to be spiritual and are working toward that goal. Rather than challenge their current way of practicing spirituality, we can connect by indicating that we also are on a spiritual journey to know God. This point came home to me after I had preached one Sunday and a young man told me he had enjoyed my "speech." His word choice let me know he was an outsider, so I asked him what had brought him to church that morning. He described feeling like he was on one side of a canyon and that God was on a cliff on the other side. I smiled to myself because the Four Spiritual Laws booklets of Campus Crusade for Christ use the same image. He said he wanted to go from his cliff to God's. After talking a bit more, I suggested that he and I form a group together, and even call it Bridges, for people to learn more about God. He loved the idea. People who are trying to develop a spiritual life won't listen to us if we begin by torpedoing their efforts.

3. Paul knew the spiritual language and culture of his audience. Churches that are growing with new young people get this principle right—not just in their verbal communi-

cation, but in their church's atmosphere, music, and communication systems, and even how they dress. That means radically different things for different places. It might mean a rodeo fellowship in South Dakota or a Crystal Cathedral in Southern California (yes, Robert Schuller Sr. was one of the first pioneers in this, even though the ministry is now defunct). Sometimes it means rock bands, and sometimes it means Gregorian chants. The important application is the need for church leaders to keep updating their understanding of the communities they are serving. Probably the most important first step is to invite the younger generations into leadership if you can, or begin by being with them on a regular basis and listening.

4. Paul then and only then bridged to the gospel, which had a mixed response. We will not have 100 percent of the people we are building bridges with walk over the bridge to faith, but we will have some.

Through a serendipitous set of circumstances, I had become the interim senior pastor of a large church in the southern suburbs of Minneapolis. I was working with the missions pastor on some of these issues, and he brought to me an idea to work with Feed My Starving Children. Frequently, the organization partners with churches and others on what they call MobilePack events at a host group's location.

Our congregation was big, so we had about 2,500 volunteers that first year. The event was successful—we packed thousands of meals. But to take it from good to great, as business consultant Jim Collins would say, the missions pastor and I talked about opening the event to outsiders. They wanted to feed starving children as much as we did, and we concluded it would be easier for our lay people to invite their friends, colleagues, and others to help feed starving children than invite them to come to worship, given the skepticism discussed in this book. I ended up preaching about this opportunity a few times before the event, and that second year we had 4,500 volunteers, a great percentage of which were not from the church. By the seventh year we were teaming up with other churches, and over ten thousand volunteers packed three million meals.

Christians and outsiders have many areas of common ground that they can work on together. We will discuss these in the methodology section of the book, but here's a starter list of common interests I have found within the Millennial generation. These won't apply to every young person, but as I said, they do reflect general areas of common ground:

- Service and giving back are a big part of this generation.
- They want to be "missionaries," without the "God-part" necessarily, by helping the needy all over the world.
- They want to make a difference with their gifts, talents, and passions.
- They want meaning and purpose in life, and will even change jobs for lesser pay in some cases to gain a sense of connection to their purpose.
- Spiritual life may involve centering, true self-connection, mindfulness, or a connection to something bigger than themselves (think devotional life here).
- Relationships with family and friends are a high priority.
- They care about social action in areas of the environment, income inequality, justice issues, etc.
- They are not, as of now, nearly as materialistic as their parents. They want *access* to things, not necessarily ownership.
- Although couples living together is common, they still think in terms of monogamous marriage someday.
- They are open to mentoring by older generations.

- They assume diversity is normal.
- They want to be world changers, and they are confident they can make it happen.
- Collaboration comes naturally, and therefore a sharing economy is very motivating to them.
- They want to learn all they can, and they are curious to experience many things.

Again, this is a preliminary list. I am sure your church can come up with some specific areas where common ground is possible.

To summarize this chapter, our segmented society began when we started to sort into "like" communities where we live. For young people, their connections and friends form a subculture online that is the true place of community for them. Through social media, they will evaluate other people and organizations through feedback from friends and other online connections, either good or bad, which causes friends to either embrace or stay away from these organizations. They think that because Christians have also become a subculture, we are out of touch, out of tune, old-fashioned, and sheltered. Millennials also believe that spirituality is vital, spiritual, and mysterious, while religion is dull, boring, lifeless, and not relevant to their lives.

We are challenged by Jesus to be salt and light and come out of our bubble to connect with outsiders in the world. This is modeled by Paul in his interaction with the Athenians, where he builds common ground. Following suit, we need to understand the communities around us, both spiritually and culturally, and affirm as much connection as we can to build trust and openness with outsiders.

Category of Revelation	What Should We Focus On?	What Question Should We Ask?
Not God	Define yourself by what you're for and not by what you're against.	Will focusing on this idea or interest resonate with or discourage people who are considering Christianity?
General Revelation	Build bridges to ideas outside Christianity, and find as much common ground as possible.	Is this idea or area of knowledge consistent with biblical teaching on this topic?
Disputable Matters in the Church	Stick to the essentials of the faith and allow for diversity on anything else where Christians disagree.	Is this topic or area of interest a disputable or indisputable matter?
The Law	Limit the requirements to engage with the faith to the very small list (4) in Acts 15.	Are we making it hard for outsiders to come to the faith?
Gospel	Focus on thirsts, hurts, and journeys rather than what is wrong with the individual.	Are we using language and concepts that will be understood by our audience?

CHAPTER 4

Disputable Matters

Accept the one whose faith is weak, without quarreling over disputable matters. One person's faith allows them to eat anything, but another, whose faith is weak, eats only vegetables. The one who eats everything must not treat with contempt the one who does not, and the one who does not eat everything must not judge the one who does, for God has accepted them. Who are you to judge someone else's servant? To their own master, servants stand or fall. And they will stand, for the Lord is able to make them stand.

One person considers one day more sacred than another; another considers every day alike. Each of them should be fully convinced in their own mind. Whoever regards one day as special does so to the Lord. Whoever eats meat does so to the Lord, for they give thanks to God; and whoever abstains does so to the Lord and gives thanks to God. For none of us lives for ourselves alone, and none of us dies for ourselves alone. If we live, we live for the Lord; and if we die, we die for the Lord. So, whether we live or die, we belong to the Lord. For this very reason, Christ died and returned to life so that he might be the Lord of both the dead and the living.

You, then, why do you judge your brother or sister? Or why do you treat them with contempt? For we will all stand before God's judgment seat. It is written:

"'As surely as I live,' says the Lord,
'every knee will bow before me;
every tongue will acknowledge God.'"

So then, each of us will give an account of ourselves to God.

Therefore let us stop passing judgment on one another. Instead, make up your mind not to put any stumbling block or obstacle in the way of a brother or sister. I am convinced, being fully persuaded in the Lord Jesus, that nothing is unclean in itself. But if anyone regards something as unclean, then for that person it is unclean. If your brother or sister is distressed because of what you eat, you are no longer acting in love. Do not by your eating destroy someone for whom Christ died. Therefore do not let what you know is good be spoken of as evil. For the kingdom of God is not a matter of eating and drinking, but of righteousness, peace and joy in the Holy Spirit, because anyone who serves Christ in this way is pleasing to God and receives human approval.

Let us therefore make every effort to do what leads to peace and to mutual edification. Do not destroy the work of God for the sake of food. All food is clean, but it is wrong for a person to eat anything that causes someone else to stumble. It is better not to eat meat or drink wine or to do anything else that will cause your brother or sister to fall.

So whatever you believe about these things keep between yourself and God. Blessed is the one who does not condemn himself by what he approves. But whoever has doubts is condemned if they eat, because their eating is not from faith; and everything that does not come from faith is sin.

We who are strong ought to bear with the failings of the weak and not to please ourselves. Each of us should please our neighbors for their good, to build them up. For even Christ did not please himself but, as it is written: "The insults of those who insult you have fallen on me." For everything that was written in the past was written to teach us, so that through the endurance taught in the Scriptures and the encouragement they provide we might have hope.

May the God who gives endurance and encouragement give you the same attitude of mind toward each other that Christ Jesus had, so that with one mind and one voice you may glorify the God and Father of our Lord Jesus Christ.

Accept one another, then, just as Christ accepted you, in order to bring praise to God.

Romans 14–15:7

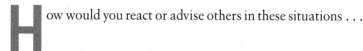

How would you react or advise others in these situations . . .

1. Imagine you are the father or mother of a young woman who is a college sophomore. She comes to you and asks what you believe about gay and lesbian issues, especially whether marriage should be allowed.

2. Picture yourself as an advisor at a youth retreat. The church's high-schoolers have brought along some of their outside friends. Around the campfire, one of the newcomers asks, "Do I need to give up smoking in order to be a follower of Jesus?"

3. Pretend for a moment that you are having lunch with a friend who is outside the church and somewhat negative about Christians. Politics comes up in your conversation, and he expresses his offense at a certain politician who speaks for Christians in general.

4. You are part of a Bible study that has invited outside friends to join the ranks. As you are deep into a discussion about a certain topic, your outside friend shares something about her lifestyle that is definitely not considered acceptable in Christian circles, and it is obvious that others are reacting in an excluding and judgmental way.

We will come back to these scenarios at the end of the chapter. Perhaps you've dealt with similar ones in your life. However, I want to look at interactions such as these through the younger generation's eyes, and analyze how they think we're doing. We will also discuss what the apostle Paul says to us in Romans 14–15. I need to say right up front that the insights I will make about these issues are within the context of the church and do not address how Christians should operate in a secular democracy. That is a completely different issue and is beyond the scope of this book. But let's begin with the cultural context of the younger generations.

I mentioned it earlier, but it's worth repeating: Tolerance almost always ranks as one of the top-three values that young people hold. They have grown up in a world where simply by using the Internet they can be in a totally different world in seconds, which defines reality for them in unique ways. For example, they know there are many answers to the questions we ask. For many, they consider it intellectually naïve to suggest that there is only one way to understand things. Also, the split of religion and spirituality in these generations has only expanded since the advent of the Internet. Consequently, the younger generation comes at religious issues with three strong tendencies:

1. Issues are not simple, and they consider people judgmental if they accuse others of being wrong about something. David Kinnaman speaks to this well: "Judgmental attitudes are particularly difficult for Mosaics (Millennials) and Busters (GenX) to swallow for two reasons. First, they are insightful about people's motives. They have been the target of endless lectures, sermons, marketing and advertisement. If you bring up unsolicited advice, they mistrust your motives. They wonder what's in it for you."[1]

2. The new generations are increasingly resistant to simplistic, black-and-white views of the world. It is a feature of the way they process life—nothing is simple. They esteem context, ambiguity, and tension. Often, judgmental

attitudes come across as oversimplified, old-fashioned, and out of step with their diverse world. With young people, how you communicate is as important as what we communicate."[2] Consequently, 87 percent of outsiders experience modern-day Christianity as judgmental in nature. *Judgmental* is defined in this case as pointing out something that is wrong in someone else's life, making the person feel put down, excluded, and marginalized.

3. Loyalty in relationships is high. Networks are the new communities for most people, and they take and appreciate feedback from others to guide decisions. They consider it disloyal to some of their connections to take a stand that seems to demean a whole class of people. Jim Wallis put it well when he said, "Young people don't want to be Left or Right. They reject these narrow political orthodoxies. They're not happy with Christianity being either a list of things you shouldn't do or just about being nice. They want to go deeper."[3]

Mistrust is built in when we approach the younger generations with a divisive focus. Only 9 percent of the young outsiders say they trust a Christian's point of view and perspective.[4]

Consequently, when we focus a huge amount of time in the church on divisive issues and black-and-white dialogue, younger people don't want any part of it. It just creates a lot of unattractive baggage about Christians in general. They carry a surprising amount of negative feelings toward us even before we start to engage with them in the culture.

We are not the first generation of Christians that has been divided over controversial issues or seen them cause churches to split. This reality goes all the way back to the disciples' time; the apostle Paul took this issue head on in Romans 14–15. Look at the text at the beginning of the chapter for a moment and then we will talk about it. Paul in his grand treatise about Christianity was addressing people in the capital of the Western world of the time, and he addressed several agenda items throughout the letter. One was the division and rancor between Jewish Christians and Gentile Christians in Rome. Paul mentioned three disputes:

1. Whether or not it was okay to drink wine or alcohol at all.
2. Whether it was okay to worship on any day of the week.
3. Whether it was okay to eat meat, or if we should all be vegetarians.

One red flag I believe we should heed is when both extremes of the church think something is not disputable. Many times that is a clue that it may fit into this category of "disputable matters." When churches disagree, I tell them that I understand they do not *think* it is disputable, but we sure are disputing about it.

Paul teaches in the book of Romans a set of behaviors that Christians are to follow in these cases:

1. In the arena of disputable matters, Christians are to be convinced in their own minds about what they believe. (14:5)
2. In the arena of disputable matters, whatever you believe about such things, keep it between you and God. (14:22)
3. Accept one another and do not quarrel over disputable matters. (14:1)
4. Each of us should please our neighbors for their good, to build them up. (15:2)
5. Make every effort to do what leads to peace and mutual edification. (14:19)
6. Do not pass judgment on one another. (14:13)

7. Make up your mind to act in love and not put any stumbling block in the way of your brother and sister. (14:13, 15)

Paul also explains the "why" behind these actions:

1. In the area of disputable matters, one person comes to a conclusion and another comes to the opposite conclusion, yet God accepts both. (14:1–3)
2. One person holds their position "to the Lord" and the other person holds their position "to the Lord." One gives thanks to the Lord for their position, and the other person gives thanks to the Lord for their position. (14:5–8)
3. In the arena of disputable matters, one person's faith leads them to one position and another person's faith leads them to the exact opposite position. *Both are in the will of God for their lives, given where their faith is at the time.* (14:14–18)
4. If we try to convince a person whose faith leads them to a different conclusion, and we cause them to doubt their faith, we pull them into sin, and we ourselves are in sin. That which is not of faith is sin. (14:19–22)

Finally, Paul points to the results in the body of Christ when we follow these radical principles:

1. We are pleasing to God and also (sometimes) win human approval. (14:18)
2. We receive peace, joy, and righteousness (right standing) before God. (14:17)
3. We find unity in diversity: "May the God who gives endurance and encouragement give you the same attitude of mind toward each other that Christ Jesus had, so that with one mind and one voice you may glorify the God and Father of our Lord Jesus Christ" (Romans 15:5–6).

These ideas may take a while to absorb because they are not talked about in most Christian circles. Paul is trying to keep the minds of these Christians focused on what is essential rather than destroying their unity and witness by trying to persuade others who are in the will of God for their lives at that moment, even if they might end up elsewhere later.

Many will push back and say, "Hold on, David, this text is talking about disputable matters. We have been discussing issues that are beyond those categories." My response is, "*I am not trying to tell you what is disputable or not disputable.* That is between you and God. What I am trying to say is the critical question before we address any issue we face is this: Is this a disputable matter or an *essential* matter to our faith?"

From there, people often ask, "How do I figure that out?" To answer that, I borrow a construct that John Wesley used in discerning theological issues that was later called the Wesleyan Quadrilateral. According to Wesley, our theological viewpoints have four inputs—Scripture, experience, reason, and tradition. Here it is in graphic form:

After working with churches across a huge theological spectrum for more than twenty years, I see four important continuums, similar to Wesley's construct, that influence our beliefs. Some people emphasize what the Bible says for a certain issue, and others, for example, place greater weight on science or personal experience. Which dimension they emphasize and where they are on the continuum of that dimension defines where they are coming from. (Note: I modify one of Wesley's dimensions by adding "science" to "reason.")

Important Continuums Across the Church as a Whole

Use of the Bible

Each word of the Bible is the Word of God—"The Bible says . . ." No outside sources are used to interpret the Bible.	The whole Bible is the Word of God—"The sweep of the Scriptures says . . ." Outside sources are used to help apply what the Bible says.	The Bible is the church book—"The themes of the Bible say . . ." Outside sources fill in themes like justice, etc.

Relationship of Scripture and Tradition

Tradition is as valid as the Bible is for wisdom and direction.	Tradition as creeds informs people, but Scripture is the ultimate authority in practice.	Tradition has no authority. The Bible itself is the only authority.

Relationship of Scripture and Science (and Reason)

Science is the enemy of Scripture, and Scripture is to be defended at all costs.	Science is important, but Scripture is the final authority, informed by and reinterpreted by science.	Science is equal with Scripture and sometimes trumps Scripture.

Relationship of Scripture and Experience

Personal experience is not important in faith and practice.	Experience is one factor among many in considering matters of faith and practice.	Experience is a very important factor in faith and practice.

When I ask Christians about issues that have been or still are divisive within the American church (alcohol, evolution, card playing, dancing, etc.), they inevitably reveal what single dimension or combination led to their beliefs (e.g., science and faith, experience and faith, how they view the Scriptures on that issue, tradition and faith).

Quite a few issues are no longer central in our culture because the culture and the church have come to see that people of good faith can disagree about them. Remember, I am talking about disputable matters in the church context, not in the secular culture context.

With many denominations and seminaries, it is not difficult to know where they stand across the board on these continuums. But when I ask pastors and others where they stand personally, they usually tell me it depends on the issue. For some, sometimes science makes a big difference in how they view an issue, sometimes not at all. Sometimes Scripture is used one way, sometimes another way. The problem is not that each of us, in Paul's language, is "convinced in our own mind" about these issues. That is the way it should be. When discussing disputable matters in the church, the problem comes when we proclaim, judge, try to argue, and change other Christians (and outsiders) to our point of view, which Paul has specifically told us not to do.

The radical principles he shares in Romans 14–15 are not, in my experience, considered or taught very much in our churches. Yet in the context of the Millennial culture, which already has a hard time believing any point of view can be definitive about anything, when we do not stick to the essentials of Christianity and allow for diversity on the nonessentials, we will find people rejecting the whole concept of Christianity altogether.

Take time and revisit four scenarios at the start of this chapter, and then consider these questions:

1. How will my answers affect the openness of outsiders to the whole idea of Christianity?
2. What response could I give or question could I ask that would not end up taking sides on disputable matters but allow for diversity of opinions in the Christian body and not derail the outsiders who are considering Christ?

3. Did your approach to any of these scenarios change significantly after considering the insights in this chapter?

I will say it again: We are not keeping the main thing the main thing. "But what is the main thing?" you may ask. Once again, that's a personal decision, but I do want to reflect on what the earlier church debated, lost their lives for, and then formalized into the first creeds of the ancient church.

The first three centuries of the Christian church, as you may know, were filled with councils where Christians were formulating in clear (often debated) words what the center of Christianity is, over and against other religious and philosophical perspectives of the day. Although the church does disagree about certain aspects of these creeds, the basic focus of these first documents involved the Trinity and the interrelationship of the Godhead. It also clarified each of the roles played by various aspects of the Trinity, with special focus on the life, death, and resurrection of Jesus Christ.

Blood was shed and believers were martyred to carve out the essentials of the faith that framed Christianity. They gave their lives to defend the core tenets of our faith, which they would not yield. They did not die for some aspect of the law, which we are debating as if it were an essential today. When we spend huge amounts of time and resources on disputable matters in the context of the church, not only are we ignoring Paul's wisdom, we take ourselves off the radar screen of most outsiders. If they do notice us, they see our internal arguments in a negative light.

In a wonderful book entitled *Essentialism: The Disciplined Pursuit of Less*, Greg McKeown discusses how people living productive, impactful, balanced lives keep to the essentials:

1. These people focus on only what is essential to the goals and objectives they are trying to achieve.
2. They say yes to only the top 10 percent of opportunities.

3. They weigh possible trade-offs if they go down a certain path (e.g., how their attention to other matters will be affected).

4. They design routines that enshrine what is essential, making execution almost effortless.[5]

We've seen principles like these work in churches. As the *Simple Church* book and movement has found, when churches focus their programming time on a few things they do very well, it causes increases in growth, stronger budgets, and involved and engaged people.[6] If we are going to engage generations where only 23 percent are even thinking about God at all, and they already perceive us as judgmental and stuck in black-white thinking, we are going to need all the resources we can muster to present the gospel contextually.

Once again, I am not going to define what is essential and nonessential for you, which I think is inappropriate. I am asking that we refocus on the essentials.

Presbyterianism has always summed up all of what I am talking about in three phrases:

In essentials, unity.

In nonessentials, diversity.

In all things, charity or love.

This generation needs to see again a Christian body that is known by its love for them in their actions and attitudes. Wouldn't it be an ingenious plan of the Enemy to get the church to focus on issue A or issue B that is part of the law, and make it so important that the church fights, divides, rejects one another, and presses their points in a very public way, so that they turn off an entire generation to the gospel of Jesus Christ and the Good News of salvation? From the outsider's perspective, that is exactly what is happening today.

Category of Revelation	What Should We Focus On?	What Question Should We Ask?
Not God	Define yourself by what you're for and not by what you're against.	Will focusing on this idea or interest resonate with or discourage people who are considering Christianity?
General Revelation	Build bridges to ideas outside Christianity, and find as much common ground as possible.	Is this idea or area of knowledge consistent with biblical teaching on this topic?
Disputable Matters in the Church	Stick to the essentials of the faith and allow for diversity on anything else where Christians disagree.	Is this topic or area of interest a disputable or indisputable matter?
The Law	Limit the requirements to engage with the faith to the very small list (4) in Acts 15.	Are we making it hard for outsiders to come to the faith?
Gospel	Focus on thirsts, hurts, and journeys rather than what is wrong with the individual.	Are we using language and concepts that will be understood by our audience?

CHAPTER 5

The Law

Certain people came down from Judea to Antioch and were teaching the believers: "Unless you are circumcised, according to the custom taught by Moses, you cannot be saved." This brought Paul and Barnabas into sharp dispute and debate with them. So Paul and Barnabas were appointed, along with some other believers, to go up to Jerusalem to see the apostles and elders about this question. The church sent them on their way, and as they traveled through Phoenicia and Samaria, they told how the Gentiles had been converted. This news made all the believers very glad. When they came to Jerusalem, they were welcomed by the church and the apostles and elders, to whom they reported everything God had done through them.

Then some of the believers who belonged to the party of the Pharisees stood up and said, "The Gentiles must be circumcised and required to keep the law of Moses."

The apostles and elders met to consider this question. After much discussion, Peter got up and addressed them: "Brothers, you know that some time ago God made a choice among you that the Gentiles might hear from my lips the message of the gospel and believe. God, who knows the heart, showed that he accepted them by giving the Holy Spirit to them, just as he did to us. He did not discriminate between us and them, for he purified their hearts by faith. Now then, why do you try to test God by putting on the necks of Gentiles a yoke that neither we nor our ancestors have been able to bear? No! We believe it is through the grace of our Lord Jesus that we are saved, just as they are."

The whole assembly became silent as they listened to Barnabas and Paul telling about the signs and wonders God had done among the Gentiles through them. When they finished, James spoke up. "Brothers," he said, "listen to me. Simon has described to us how God first intervened to choose a people for his name from the Gentiles. The words of the prophets are in agreement with this, as it is written:

> "'After this I will return
> and rebuild David's fallen tent.
> Its ruins I will rebuild,
> and I will restore it,
> that the rest of mankind may seek the Lord,
> even all the Gentiles who bear my name,
> says the Lord, who does these things'—
> things known from long ago.

"It is my judgment, therefore, that we should not make it difficult for the Gentiles who are turning to God. Instead we should write to them, telling them to abstain from food polluted by idols, from sexual immorality, from the meat of strangled animals and from blood. For the law of Moses has been preached in every city from the earliest times and is read in the synagogues on every Sabbath."

Acts 15:1–21

was talking about this book to a friend of mine whom I see once a month, and mentioned the building of common ground around our church's Feed My Starving Children campaign. "I would love to do Jesus-like things with Christians around me," he said. "Maybe then they will stop telling me what is wrong with me." There is so much wrapped up in that two-sentence encounter, and this chapter will talk about engaging younger generations around what we typically call the law.

There seems to be a disconnect between the love Jesus emphasizes and how we live out our faith. In a Barna Group study for Freedom in Christ Ministries, they explored the perspectives that Christian churchgoers have in any given month:

> More than four out of five agreed the Christian life is well described as "trying harder to do what God commands." Two-thirds of churchgoers said, "Rigid rules and strict standards are an important part of the life and teaching of my church." Three out of every five churchgoers in America feel that they "do not measure up to God's standards." And one-quarter admitted that they serve God out of a sense of "guilt and obligation rather than joy and gratitude."[1]

What happens when we emphasize the law in church? First, many of us start to believe that outsiders are not drawn to Christianity because they can't cut it morally (which, in actuality, is not even a top-five reason). Second, there is a tendency to feel morally superior to those around us.

Here is what David Kinnaman found as a result of using what he calls "lifestyle points" (i.e., following rules and regulations) as our benchmark to measuring how Christian we are:

> The gospel—the good news of Jesus Christ—is that God has released us from striving to measure up to God's standards, let alone the expectations of other human beings. In a culture where some moral values are slipping with the new generation, we assume the best way to right the ship is to fix the morals. In this context, what are Christians known for? Outsiders think of our moralizing, our condemnations, and our attempt to draw boundaries around everything. Even if the standards are accurate and biblical, they seem to be all we offer. And our lives are a poor advertisement (almost no difference in many measures) to these standards. We have set the game board to register lifestyle points, then we are surprised to be trapped by our own mistakes. The truth is we have invited the hypocrite image on ourselves.[2]

Hard stuff to hear, but it lines up with my experience. One of my best friends was good friends with a couple who lives near us. They did many things together because their kids participated in the same events. It was a great relationship for both couples. My friend's wife applied for a job at a Christian business close by and listed this couple, among others, as a character reference. Later, it was explained to her that she was rejected for the job because one of her character references had given a bad report about all the ways she was not measuring up to God's standard. As you might expect, my friend felt betrayed and condemned.

This was an extreme situation, but these sorts of thing happen when we begin to measure each other's righteousness according to our own, often narrow, criterion. What outsiders pick up is a "holier than thou" attitude over what they see as insignificant differences. This is definitely not love.

A great book about Millennials, written by a Millennial, is *Fast Future* by David Burstein. He says his peers have grown up in a world that futurists call VUCA—volatile, uncertain, complex, and ambiguous. They have lived through 9/11, two wars, the impeachment of a president, politics of personal destruction, the devastation of families, jobs, and homes, a dysfunctional financial system, the mega-collapse of companies and national economies, America's debt burden, and hurricane Katrina, to name just a few. Their formative years have taught them that resilience and adaptability are essential to survival.

> We scarcely notice the overall dissolution of authority in society, the collapse of institutions, the increasing level of complexity and the inability of existing systems to manage through it and solve problems. Rapid change is the only constant. And the chief survival skill of the Millennials is keeping our balance in this sometimes mad, sometimes surreal, always changing topsy-turvy world.[3]

Morality in this context is becoming more and more emotive, a term used for modern moral decision-making. Emotivism is a technical philosophy that believes that all moral judgments are simply expressions of emotion and preference, and not statements of facts or first principles. To younger generations, judgmental statements (think the law here) often come across as "oversimplified, old-fashioned, and out of step with their diverse world."[4] On top of this, they have the confidence to challenge authority, not taking a statement like "the Bible says" as definitive at all. Their whole understanding of the spiritual life as a journey that is guided by the best instincts of your heart is a very common way of moving through the moral complexity they experience.

When I listen to people processing their lives from a spiritual point of view outside of the church, the language they use points to this individual, creative point of view. One group of people were discussing a crossroads in their lives, and the most important criterion for moving forward was "expressing your true self" or "going with your heart" or being "you." All this language suggests that the supreme guidance system for all people is their internal compass, informed by a whole lifetime of experiences, inputs, personal preferences, and life choices. Moral absolutes seem completely out of tune with this way of being in the world.

To bring all this together, currently we have set up a system that awards "lifestyle points" for following the law, therefore rules and regulations are how most churchgoers (four out of five, if you recall) experience Christianity at the moment. This transfers into outsiders believing Christians are all about rules and regulations and nothing else. Meanwhile, the younger generations are responding to the VUCA world of volatility, uncertainty, complexity, and ambiguity, and consider it a great virtue to be able to be flexible and adaptable in a changing environment. They see life and the spiritual life as a journey and, for the most part, do not accept the Bible as valid or immediately applicable in their situation, let alone everyone else's.

How Did This Look to the Apostles?

In an interesting parallel, Jesus accused the religious people of his day (think us, today) of loading up the "backpacks" of ordinary people with the law and its rules and regulations. Talking to a crowd, Jesus called out the Pharisees: "They say things and do not do them. They tie up heavy burdens and lay them on men's shoulders, but they are unwilling to move them with so much as a finger" (Matthew 23:3–4 NASB). This made the Pharisees "twice as fit for hell," as Jesus put it (Matthew 23:15 CEV). These are some of his strongest words in all the Gospels.

The apostles struggled to understand law and grace all the way through the New Testament (including Romans, Galatians,

1 Peter, and James). Concerning outsiders (Gentiles, in their context), they came to a unanimous decision in the Council of Jerusalem recorded in Acts 15.

At that time the apostles were in sharp dispute about whether the Gentiles should be shouldering the law after they were converted, especially represented by circumcision. It became so heated that they brought all the apostles together to grapple with this issue. Paul and Barnabas spoke, Peter testified, and finally James uttered these pivotal words:

> We should not make it difficult for the Gentiles who are turning to God.

Acts 15:19

Now, the apostles talked a lot in their letters to believers about following Christ, about what the kingdom of God was like, and what the kingdom of God was not like, but all of that was aimed toward the church. They mentioned repentance from sin when they were sharing the gospel, but it was done carefully, building on the positive things this would do in the outsider's life, so if they were offended, it would be the gospel itself that offended them. We know that the incredible evangelistic explosion in those first centuries was sparked by the love, service, and sacrifice of the Christians on behalf of people around them. And the demonstrated grace spread like wildfire.

I want to suggest three reasons why the apostles came to the conclusion they did about the law.

First, from their time with Jesus they understood that there are stages in the Christian life. (Paul referred to certain basic teachings of the faith as "milk" and deeper doctrines as "meat," and John talked about children of the faith, young people of the faith, and elders in the faith.) In the parable of the sower, Jesus illustrated the progression of the Christian life. First, the seed needed to penetrate a hard heart. Second, the rocks in a person's life needed to be attended to so that the root systems could get to the nourishment of the love of God. Then, the thorns (think the law, deceitfulness of riches, the desire for other things) were to be addressed. Paul also used an agricultural image when he said people are to be rooted and grounded in God's love. The interesting thing in both Hebrews and in 1 Corinthians is that Paul is unwilling to move off the milk of the Word and the elemental things in Hebrews until they have had their effect. To use an image from any training context, beginners are not asked to pull off the same feats that seasoned athletes, musicians, and artists do, because they have not yet mastered the craft. Mastery takes ten thousand hours, as Malcolm Gladwell says in his book *Outliers*. The exact number has been debated, but the point remains: It takes time to grow and develop in the Christian faith.

Second, after Christians are rooted in God's love, acceptance, and forgiveness, the Holy Spirit begins to change their hearts. As Christians respond to the Holy Spirit's guidance, they become motivated to change aspects of their character, behavior, and values. A desire grows to be "slaves to righteousness," as Paul says in Romans 6:18. With a changed heart, a person is motivated to pursue goodness, self-control, and other qualities that will keep them from being "ineffective and unproductive" (2 Peter 1:8).

Philippians 2:1–2 says it well: "Therefore if you have any encouragement from being united with Christ, if any comfort from his love, if any common sharing in the Spirit, if any tenderness and compassion, then make my joy complete by being like-minded, having the same love . . . and of one mind." That is a big IF. People outside the grace of God may be motivated to follow some of what we call the law, but our fundamental reasons come out of ongoing encounters with God.

Third, and most important in the context of this book, our current law-centric approach to sharing the Good News is having a reverse effect. We've touched on this before, but instead of bringing people closer to considering the claims of Christ, it is building up a backpack of resentment and negative orientations to the entire idea of Christianity.

As the apostles considered the whole law, they came back to the foundational question: Is this going to make it hard for the Gentiles to come to faith? James voiced only four restrictions: "We should write to them, telling them to abstain from food polluted by idols, from sexual immorality, from the meat of strangled animals and from blood" (Acts 15:20).

We are coming across as rule-followers, and there is an expectation that the outsiders need to follow the rules before they will be accepted and be part of our club.

Here are some practical suggestions for our ministries and churches:

1. Always ask the question the apostles asked: Are we making it hard for the Gentiles to come to faith?
2. Throw the lists away—or make them very, very small—when it comes to requirements of outsiders when they are simply considering the Good News of the gospel.
3. Do not lead with the law when you are with outsiders, because young people already believe that rules, etc., are all we are about anyway.
4. Remember the gospel is good news to a broken, thirsty, needy world—for us and for them.
5. Keep the great commandments front and center in everything you do. Ask, is such-and-such causing me to love God and love people more, or is it working against that possibility?

This represents a sea of change for many Christians and churches today. Sometimes, not even intentionally, people are seeing "rules and law" as they look at what is going on in our lives and our churches. My strongest point of pain over the last few decades has been watching Christians of all stripes try to force a morality on outsider populations. This has caused a vast majority to already have a negative impression, or to get their radar up and defenses locked in place when we try, as Christians, to influence them in a direction where they can know the God of love.

Category of Revelation	What Should We Focus On?	What Question Should We Ask?
Not God	Define yourself by what you're for and not by what you're against.	Will focusing on this idea or interest resonate with or discourage people who are considering Christianity?
General Revelation	Build bridges to ideas outside Christianity, and find as much common ground as possible.	Is this idea or area of knowledge consistent with biblical teaching on this topic?
Disputable Matters in the Church	Stick to the essentials of the faith and allow for diversity on anything else where Christians disagree.	Is this topic or area of interest a disputable or non-disputable matter?
The Law	Limit the requirements to engage with the faith to the very small list (4) in Acts 15.	Are we making it hard for outsiders to come to the faith?
Gospel	Focus on thirsts, hurts, and journeys rather than what is wrong with the individual.	Are we using language and concepts that will be understood by our audience?

CHAPTER 6

The Gospel

That same day two of them were walking to the village Emmaus, about seven miles out of Jerusalem. They were deep in conversation, going over all these things that had happened. In the middle of their talk and questions, Jesus came up and walked along with them. But they were not able to recognize who he was.

He asked, "What's this you're discussing so intently as you walk along?"

They just stood there, long-faced, like they had lost their best friend. Then one of them, his name was Cleopas, said, "Are you the only one in Jerusalem who hasn't heard what's happened during the last few days?"

He said, "What has happened?"

They said, "The things that happened to Jesus the Nazarene. He was a man of God, a prophet, dynamic in work and word, blessed by both God and all the people. Then our high priests and leaders betrayed him, got him sentenced to death, and crucified him. And we had our hopes up that he was the One, the One about to deliver Israel. And it is now the third day since it happened. But now some of our women have completely confused us. Early this morning they were at the tomb and couldn't find his body. They came back with the story that they had seen a vision of angels who said he was alive. Some of our friends went off to the tomb to check and found it empty just as the women said, but they didn't see Jesus."

Then he said to them, "So thick-headed! So slow-hearted! Why can't you simply believe all that the prophets said? Don't you see that these things had to happen, that the Messiah had to suffer and only then enter into his glory?" Then he started at the beginning, with the Books of Moses, and went on through all the Prophets, pointing out everything in the Scriptures that referred to him.

They came to the edge of the village where they were headed. He acted as if he were going on but they pressed him: "Stay and have supper with us. It's nearly evening; the day is done." So he went in with them. And here is what happened: He sat down at the table with them. Taking the bread, he blessed and broke and gave it to them. At that moment, open-eyed, wide-eyed, they recognized him. And then he disappeared.

Back and forth they talked. "Didn't we feel on fire as he conversed with us on the road, as he opened up the Scriptures for us?"

Luke 24:13–32 The Message

f there is one thing that most Christians agree with, it is the centrality of the gospel. As Paul put it in Romans, "It is the power of God that brings salvation to everyone who believes: first to the Jew, then to the Gentile" (1:16). What may be surprising is how many Americans have been drawn to the gospel at some point in their journeys. Some statistics from Kinnaman's studies: 82 percent of the population has "test-driven" Christianity at one time in their lives (meaning they have gone to a Christian church at least once), and 65 percent of Americans have made a commitment to Christ.[1] In *Vanishing Grace*, Philip Yancey wrote about a friend who worked at a coffee shop. The friend noticed that "post-Christians," people who had once been involved with Christianity, now "harbored bad feelings. Some carried memories of past wounds: a church split, a domineering parent, a youth director or priest guilty of sexual abuse, a nasty divorce that the church handled clumsily. Others had simply absorbed the media's negative stereotypes of rabid fundamentalists and scandal-prone television evangelists."[2]

Three-quarters of young outsiders qualify as post-Christian. I have become keenly aware of this reality in my work with churches over the years. When I ask about adult children or grandchildren going to church, most heads drop to their chests in embarrassment or despair.

So why has this happened?

The first level of barriers comes from how, aggregately, we are approaching outsiders. Many experience us as spiritual head-hunters who simply are trying to get people saved but don't really care about them as individuals. Millennials, as we have discussed, can smell people's motives a mile away. In interviews, people told me about their experiences with Christians: "They don't really listen to me because they are simply preparing their rebuttal, even before they know my story. . . . Even in Bible studies I have tried to join, I feel judged just because I am an outsider. . . . I often sense that my spiritual experience is considered bad because it is not their particular experience. . . . They tend to point out what is wrong with me, and have a hard time actually addressing my questions. . . . I often get simple answers in this complex world that convince me they are not dealing with the deep reality of most issues. . . ." This causes two-thirds of outsiders to believe we are not authentic about our interactions with them. Interestingly, two-thirds of Christians believe that outsiders would say we are genuine.[3]

Furthermore, the younger generations are motivated by connection, interaction, experience, and participation, supported by a resolute individualism that gives them the self-confidence to question anything to test its validity, only buying in when it resonates with them. I have heard many young people say that words don't mean anything in and of themselves.

What does all of this add up to? It means that you can assume that most outsiders have negative baggage toward the church and are skeptical of Christianity.

Jesus had many approaches with outsiders, but one in particular is symbolic, in my opinion, of where we are today in America. It is the well-known story called the Road to Emmaus, which led off this chapter. We will retrace this story one step at a time, and talk about its application to our situation today.

First of all, notice that Jesus joined these disciples in a discussion that was already going on. They were talking about that day's news of Jesus, his death, and his rumored resurrection. He started by walking alongside them, simply listening to their conversation rather than starting with his own agenda. The disciples were processing together what happened these last few days, clearly discouraged and confused. That is a good description of most of the post-Christians in America today, as we have seen.

Jesus then asks what they are discussing. His question surprised them. *Was he the only person in Jerusalem who didn't know what had happened?* Similarly, as we have learned, many outsiders believe we are ignorant, out of touch, and not in tune with the twenty-first century. The great irony, of course, is that Jesus is actually the only one who knew the full picture of what was happening in Jerusalem in those days. Rather than push back, he inquires deeper about the disciples' thoughts and experiences.

Everyone around us has a story, and most have interacted with Jesus and Christianity as part of that story. In this case of the disciples, they talked about their beliefs in Jesus, how the religious elite had killed him, and how this dashed their hopes. They also expressed their confusion about the women who witnessed the resurrection, even though the disciples did see an empty tomb but not Jesus. I find it almost always true that outsiders need to express to Christians, in some form, all the bad, confusing, or discouraging experiences they have had with Christianity before they are open to a new possibility.

From there, Jesus begins to engage their doubt and unbelief with in-depth answers from the Old Testament of why he needed to suffer, die, and rise from the dead. No pat answers were given. Instead it was a full response to their questions, doubts, and discouragements. It was also the verification of the Holy Spirit internally that was also taking this beyond just words and into experience.

I like what happens next. Jesus "continued on as if he were going further." He has his audience excited but chooses to act like he is moving on. Why? We can only speculate, but I believe he will not force them to go further until they want to go deeper, until they have decided they want to learn and experience more. He clearly is focused on the process of their understanding, and not just the product of their belief in him. For a majority of adults, reexamining Christianity will not be one exposure to something different, but a journey together with Christians.

On the road to Emmaus, the men ask Jesus to have dinner and interact with them more. When he breaks bread, their eyes are opened and they see it for themselves. It is through a deeper relationship with Jesus over dinner, and maybe the obvious repeating of the Last Supper context, that they recognize him.

The other conundrum is, now that they believe in him, why would he disappear? I think it is because the Holy Spirit is now inside of them affirming their belief, so he does not need to be physically with them any longer. This type of personal experience, after interacting and developing a relationship with Christians, speaks to the need in the younger generations to experience it for themselves, given their resolute individualism. The end of the story is wonderful as they hurry back to Jerusalem to tell the apostles. The good news about the younger generations is the reality that they will share the news with one another. That is what they love to do—share their experiences.

Important guidelines for sharing the gospel and the kingdom of God come from this encounter with Jesus.

1. We need to know what outsiders are talking about, and where they are on their journey, before we speak. They need to know we genuinely care about them. This came home to me when I was talking to one of my good friends, who was not a Christian, and who knew me before I was. He was asking some great questions about Christianity,

one of which required that I go into some biblical texts to answer his question well. I asked him if he wanted to talk about this further, because I would need to come from a biblical point of view. He said to me, "Yes I do, if you will commit to me one thing—that you will still be my friend even if I never follow the Christian faith like you do." That puts this whole thing in a nutshell. Authenticity and genuine care are always critical in our relationships, but especially when interacting with generations who see through bad motives quickly.

2. We need to understand the younger generations around us, and more personally, about individual people interacting with us. The gospel and the kingdom of God are, for most, a "been there, done that" experience, so our creativity and relevance to their lives are very important if we are to be taken seriously.

3. Take time to give in-depth answers to their questions, knowing that they are aware every day that people have very different answers than we do to life's central questions. Using phrases like "in my opinion" and "from my perspective" and "what do you think" are critical to having a conversation, not giving a lecture.

4. Give people time to step back and consider whether they want to talk further now, or perhaps at a different time. They need to feel that they are always free to disagree or walk away for now, like normal relationships around them. Don't make their response at a certain moment jeopardize the relationship from your side, although it may turn out to be a deal breaker from their side.

5. Realize it is almost always deeper relationship that gives the Holy Spirit time to work and create the atmosphere for people to consider following Christ. Few people, percentage-wise, come to Christ through televangelists

and a media-driven gospel (less than 2 percent). It has always been friends and relationships (close to 45 percent) that are the major conduit of people considering following Christ, with the next closest (16 percent) being their own action.[4]

6. The great news, for followers of Christ, is that Millennials will figure out a way to share this with others around them.

Bringing It Together

As we finish the first part of this book, I want to summarize what we have covered before we start discussing methodologies.

My first premise is the need for a very different mindset, attitude, and behavioral pattern for a great many churches in America if we are going to engage outsiders with the claims of Christ. Unfortunately, we have actually been driving them away with what we normally emphasize (the law, morals, etc.).

Second, Jesus and the apostles knew the centrality of the gospel and the kingdom of God, and prioritized it above all things, which caused them to approach outsiders very differently from those who already knew God and were devoted followers of Christ—those who had "tasted the goodness of the word of God" (Hebrews 6:5). They looked through the lens to determine which part of God's revelation they were talking about in handling issues, priorities, and behaviors toward those outside the faith.

In the chart that has been shown repeatedly, the five categories of God's revelation are presented, along with the questions that informed the apostles before they would engage any topic, as well as a one-sentence summary of how to approach this category for those of us who are followers today. I have also tried to contextualize each of these parts of God's revelation, especially how young outsiders in America today are experiencing things from the church and Christians, as well as given opening principles on how to approach each category differently.

Here is the great news. Many churches are applying these principles well in their situations, and are being successful with the younger generations. The second half of this book is all about the methodologies that churches are using to accomplish this within their contexts. My hope in the second half of the book is to give you one way to look at the whole picture of what is happening, and not just one church's model. It is my experience that the Holy Spirit will contextualize the actual strategy to the specific environments, church histories, gifts and talents, and passions of individual churches. Therefore, merely adopting someone else's model is not the way forward. In fact, adopting a model can be dangerous if you do not share many things in common with the context in which it has worked.

Still, models are important for the church in this sense. They spark the imagination of other church leaders, borrowing bits and pieces from many different models that can be recombined for the customized strategy of a particular environment. Therefore, you will see me describing some of the popular models out in the marketplace today for that purpose. I also will be referring back to what we have covered so far, and applying that to the methodologies that follow. For now, though, it is not only possible, but actually happening for churches to adapt their strategy and mindset for future generations. Now, let's proceed to the methodologies.

PART TWO

METHODOLOGY

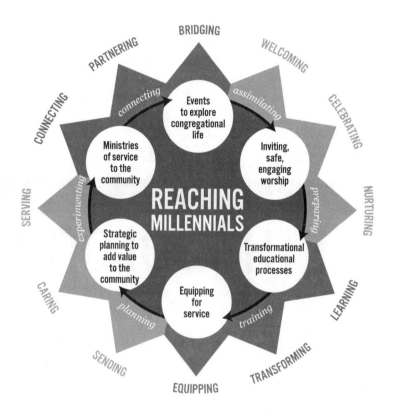

CHAPTER 7

Essentials-Based Church

Son of man, describe the temple to the people of Israel, that they may be ashamed of their sins. Let them consider its perfection, and if they are ashamed of all they have done, make known to them the design of the temple—its arrangement, its exits and entrances—its whole design and all its regulations and laws

Ezekiel 43:10–11

The man brought me back to the entrance of the temple, and I saw water coming out from under the threshold of the temple toward the east (for the temple faced east). The water was coming down from under the south side of the temple, south of the altar. He then brought me out through the north gate and led me around the outside to the outer gate facing east, and the water was trickling from the south side.

As the man went eastward with a measuring line in his hand, he measured off a thousand cubits and then led me through water that was ankle-deep. He measured off another thousand cubits and led me through water that was knee-deep. He measured off another thousand and led me through water that was up to the waist. He measured off another thousand, but now it was a river that I could not cross, because the water had risen and was deep enough to swim in—a river that no one could cross. He asked me, "Son of man, do you see this?"

Then he led me back to the bank of the river. When I arrived there, I saw a great number of trees on each side of the river. He said to me, "This water flows toward the eastern region and goes down into the Arabah, where it enters the Dead Sea. When it empties into the sea, the salty water there becomes fresh. Swarms of living creatures will live wherever the river flows. There will be large numbers of fish, because this water flows there and makes the salt water fresh; so where the river flows everything will live. Fishermen will stand along the shore; from En Gedi to En Eglaim there will be places for spreading nets. The fish will be of many kinds—like the fish of the Mediterranean Sea. But the swamps and marshes will not become fresh; they will be left for salt. Fruit trees of all kinds will grow on both banks of the river. Their leaves will not wither, nor will their fruit fail. Every month they will bear fruit, because the water from the sanctuary flows to them. Their fruit will serve for food and their leaves for healing."

Ezekiel 47:1–12

For all the challenges in reaching American Millennials, there is a growing crisis in Europe, where more and more church properties in towns and cities are being repurposed. This issue is understandably emotional for many, because these churches were once the center of community life for much of the European continent.

I saw the extent of secularization in parts of Europe when I visited my son in the Czech Republic a few years ago. He had a great semester abroad, and our family had a chance to visit him before he came home. His guest parents had been wonderful to him. They took us to dinner and we listened to beautiful music at a festival in the city we were visiting. At dinner, his guest mom asked me a surprising question: "Can you tell me what a minister is and does? I have no concept of what that means." I had never been asked that up to that time, but it revealed the little she had been exposed to the idea of church, Christianity, and faith. She did not ask it with any malice at all; my profession just seemed like a strange curiosity to her.

Her question has stuck in my heart since that day; I am very aware that America is moving quickly in Europe's direction. As I mentioned, it is common for me to talk to church leaders and find out that over 80 percent of their congregations are dying, numerically speaking. Let me share an illustration that I have used many times.

My earliest job out of college was managing a greenhouse nursery. The wonderful and stressful part of working with living things is the need to never take your eyes off of them for very long because things can go south very fast. In working with plants, two concepts you need to know are their temporary wilting point and their permanent wilting point. Plants all go through a temporary wilting point when they are stressed and not enough water has been supplied to keep them alive. The permanent wilting point happens when the plant is going to die, no matter how you tend to it.

The population of congregations in the United States is diminishing. There are about 350,000 churches in the U.S., and most draw fewer than two hundred worshipers. Of course, this is not the first time the church has had to rethink its ministry methods. But a vast majority of churches need to act so that we do not have a closing of massive numbers of congregations. The hardest thing for me to watch is well-intentioned pastors and lay leaders seeing discouraging results, diminished expectations, and many times diminishing budgets and attendance.

Since the beginning of my ministry, God has used different texts in Ezekiel to influence my work, and the text early in this chapter has been the central one. It is a vision Ezekiel had as Israel was returning from exile. The people were exiled by their continual rebellion over many decades, in order to allow God to be God in their midst. In this passage, as God is doing a new thing with the nation, a new description of the temple is recorded. It does not fit any other pattern of the temple given before this point in Israel. In other words, God uses new structures for new times.

God has impressed on many people in the church that we need a new structure to minister into a new time in our culture—new wineskins, as Jesus puts it in the New Testament. What has captured my attention that is completely different from other descriptions of the temple in the Old Testament is the goal being focused toward the outsiders, as the river flows into the dry land (arid desert land) to bring life, healing, and renewal. In our settings, what is often termed *missional* is the turning of the church back into the world to do these same things. It will require us to rethink foundational things about how we do things, both theologically and methodologically.

The good news is this is a very creative time in the church, and some congregations are thriving and representing the gospel to a skeptical and indifferent culture. In this part of the book, I am going to develop a way of viewing how the church has responded to this new cultural environment over the last few decades, broadly, and how churches have used the principles I have developed in the first part of the book with effectiveness across very different environments. I will be introducing you to an understanding of church life I find very useful in order to capture, on a high level, what is happening in the church in America today.

But before I describe this system, I ask that you keep the following in mind as you read on.

1. **This discussion is only a starting point.** As I have described this system to many pastors, I have watched the lights go on in their heads about what they see around them. Bringing this clarity is the first thing I want to communicate, but it will not be an exhaustive description, just a starting point. One pastor described this system as very catalytic for him, and I hope that is exactly what it is for you.

2. **It is a representative gallery.** My mother is an art expert and for years ran the education side of the Denver Art Museum. It is so fun to walk through museums with her; it is like having your own professor to help you under-

stand what you are looking at and what the art's relevance is. When I was in seminary at Princeton, she came back and took us through the Princeton University art gallery, which she described as a representative gallery, meaning they have one or two wonderful pieces representing different artistic styles and genres. I am going to use this style in the chapters that follow. I will use a representative church in each of the four quadrants you will learn about so you can see the basic outline of how these churches have worked and are continuing to work. I won't use specific churches, because they vary drastically. This will, however, give you a sense of how churches have responded to the fact that younger generations are, for the most part, not seeking out the church for their spiritual lives.

3. **There is also an online platform.** To provide more detail and have a community where people are adding content all the time, I have built a platform at www.represent.church. You will see a wide variety of possibilities on this site as well as ways to contribute or interact with other churches facing these same realities. I hope you will join the community and be part of this developing understanding of church life going forward.

4. **It is structured to bring clarity, not to be comprehensive.** At the beginning of this chapter was a diagram. You will notice that I broke down church ministries and programs into systems. Every church has a way of welcoming people to the church and celebration and worship services of all kinds. Also, churches nurture people into involvement in the church, where learning happens all the way from diapers to the elderly. Transformational systems involving small groups, mentoring, spiritual formation workshops, and other processes are one of the best methods

for spiritual growth. They also facilitate the equipping of lay leaders and members to be involved in the ministry and mission of the church.

In the middle part of the twentieth century, the right half of the diagram was most of what churches were doing because a majority of people in America defined their spiritual lives through churches and synagogues. That all changed over the past few decades, so I have drawn the left half of the circle to focus on what many have called externally focused churches. In these cases, churches send people to care and serve in the community, where they make connections with outsiders, establishing partnerships with them in order to attract some to becoming involved in the church. The importance of this way of understanding churches is its flexibility and clarity about any given church, regardless of theology, denomination, or regional location.

One more resource will help you understand the structure of the next few chapters. I find that dividing this diagram into four quadrants is the best way to describe the responses of churches in the wide sense of the whole American expression of congregations. I have had the chance to work with dozens of denominations over twenty years, and this is the way I can bring some order to what is happening. The four-quadrant picture is shown on the next page.

Any single church model may incorporate multiple parts or some combination of these characteristics, but I find that these will help explain what the many unique expressions of responding to outsiders look like. I will be developing a chapter on each of these quadrants in this methodological section. Each chapter will introduce what I mean by each of these categories, and offer examples of how each of these look in different environments. I will also be incorporating a discussion of trends among the

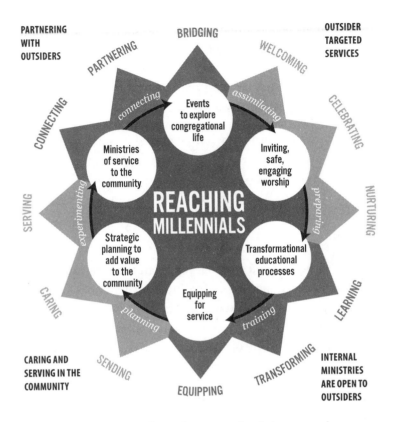

younger generations that relate to each of these quadrants, as well as how the principles from the first half of the book are incorporated into these responses.

A few additional thoughts before we move forward:

Don't get overwhelmed. Churches can begin with a few changes and add others as the contextualized application emerges for them. These responses took time in every one of the contexts in which they were developed. In fact, the process of developing is as critical as the eventual result because of the critical learning and changing that happen as the leaders of a church embark on this journey.

Involve young people around you in understanding these trends. Perhaps the most important first step is to make sure young people are engaged with you from the very beginning. They understand through their experiences and foundations what these principles mean in your context.

Your church has probably been engaged in some of this already. In these chapters, we are simply highlighting and giving a basic structure to what many churches have been doing for a long time. We are going to bring some clarity about what this means in terms of outsiders and reengaging younger generations.

Visit churches around you that represent these various quadrants. In many communities there are churches that are already applying this to their situations. The best way to get a good understanding is to go to their worship services and talk to their leaders and staff. It will open up your understanding so you can see the context and how it is being applied already.

Don't adopt someone else's model. One thing I want to say upfront, something successful churches also credit, is it takes an iterative and evolutionary process to discover a good model for reaching Millennials. Models do help give us ideas for our context, showing us ways to actually implement various ministries and programs. But the work of each set of leaders in their context must be worked out within their own vision, their own history, and their own environment. I have seen many "adopt the model" churches where it did not work in their environment because they should have adopted the principles and ideas but tailored them to their unique setting.

Don't do it alone. This is definitely a team effort for many reasons. Whenever I consult with churches on this journey, I immediately develop a team of people who will be working together.

I am hopeful that many churches can begin this journey and see a new future with vitality and growth over the next decade. But it is time to keep the main thing the main thing—helping local churches thrive.

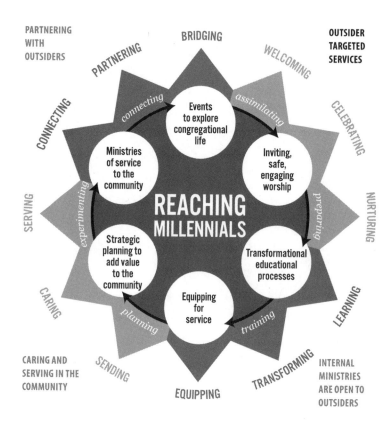

PARTNERING
WITH
OUTSIDERS

BRIDGING

OUTSIDER
TARGETED
SERVICES

PARTNERING

WELCOMING

CONNECTING

CELEBRATING

connecting

Events
to explore
congregational
life

assimilating

Ministries
of service
to the
community

Inviting,
safe,
engaging
worship

SERVING

REACHING
MILLENNIALS

NURTURING

experimenting

preparing

Strategic
planning to
add value
to the
community

Transformational
educational
processes

CARING

Equipping
for
service

LEARNING

planning

training

CARING AND
SERVING IN THE
COMMUNITY

SENDING

EQUIPPING

TRANSFORMING

INTERNAL
MINISTRIES
ARE OPEN TO
OUTSIDERS

CHAPTER 8

Outsider Targeted Services

Jesus entered Jericho and was passing through. A man was there by the name of Zacchaeus; he was a chief tax collector and was wealthy. He wanted to see who Jesus was, but because he was short he could not see over the crowd. So he ran ahead and climbed a sycamore-fig tree to see him, since Jesus was coming that way.

When Jesus reached the spot, he looked up and said to him, "Zacchaeus, come down immediately. I must stay at your house today." So he came down at once and welcomed him gladly.

All the people saw this and began to mutter, "He has gone to be the guest of a sinner."

But Zacchaeus stood up and said to the Lord, "Look, Lord! Here and now I give half of my possessions to the poor, and if I have cheated anybody out of anything, I will pay back four times the amount."

Jesus said to him, "Today salvation has come to this house, because this man, too, is a son of Abraham. For the Son of Man came to seek and to save the lost."

Luke 19:1–10

After [the younger son] had spent everything, there was a severe famine in that whole country, and he began to be in need. So he went and hired himself out to a citizen of that country, who sent him to his fields to feed pigs. He longed to fill his stomach with the pods that the pigs were eating, but no one gave him anything.

When he came to his senses, he said, "How many of my father's hired servants have food to spare, and here I am starving to death! I will set out and go back to my father and say to him: Father, I have sinned against heaven and against you. I am no longer worthy to be called your son; make me like one of your hired servants." So he got up and went to his father.

But while he was still a long way off, his father saw him and was filled with compassion for him; he ran to his son, threw his arms around him and kissed him.

The son said to him, "Father, I have sinned against heaven and against you. I am no longer worthy to be called your son."

But the father said to his servants, "Quick! Bring the best robe and put it on him. Put a ring on his finger and sandals on his feet. Bring the fattened calf and kill it. Let's have a feast and celebrate. For this son of mine was dead and is alive again; he was lost and is found." So they began to celebrate.

Luke 15:14–24

As you have read, I have had the chance to work with a lot of churches in my ministry over the past couple of decades, and pastors frequently confide in me how hard it is to keep the children or grandchildren of their members coming to church. As I probe deeper, I inquire whether these young people have stopped going altogether or have just stopped attending *their* church. A good percentage had stopped going altogether, but others were now attending the "new" church in town—one that seemed to be packed with young people. The pastor always asks me why.

I want to tackle one of the most common reasons behind young people leaving churches, a phenomenon that has been going on for three decades or so in America. To answer this question I will focus on "Outsider Targeted Services," or the three systems in the upper right-hand quadrant of the diagram: the Welcoming, Celebrating (worship), and Nurturing systems of churches. Many new churches have changed these three systems in order to respond to the younger generations.

Many church leaders think it's all about "screens"—having a video component in the service. While there are many models, it is *not* only about screens. In fact, screens may be involved, but the central idea gets more deeply into the different approaches in the three systems mentioned above, which we will take one at a time. Before we do that, however, we need to talk about how to get young people to your front door.

Your "Front Door"

Why, you may ask, do I want to talk about your front door? Well, first of all, for Millennials, your front door is not the actual main door to your building. The Millennial generation, like all digital natives, will always use your website as the front door, even if it is just to find out the time of your church services. You should assume that nearly 100 percent of all outsiders will look at the website first before attending your church. Consequently, it is critical to gear the front page of your website so outsiders can understand it and navigate it easily. Many churches will have an "I'm new here" page dedicated to new people.

In many cases they will also vet you through friends in their social networks, so begin to think about having a social presence. This, in effect, meets outsiders where they live. Also, many times they will listen to podcasts of sermons or look at pictures on your website to see what kind of people attend your church. Their online activities do not stop there. They want to continue to connect online as part of the community. Many churches now have a voluntary or paid staff position for digital and social communications, because that is where your members and outsiders are living.

But those are just some of the realities of connecting today. Here is a summary list of what you can assume with most Millennials in the areas of welcoming, worshiping, and nurturing them into the life of the church:

1. The front door to your church is your website, vetted through social networks.

2. Flowing back and forth from engagement to disengagement is the reality of every other aspect of their lives, so you shouldn't assume they will attend regularly.

3. Watching a simulcast on their devices does not seem like an inferior choice to many of them, in comparison to meeting face to face.

4. Face-to-face meetings are precious and saved for the most important get-togethers in their lives.

5. They are used to giving feedback about everything, and therefore listening to what they may consider a monologue for twenty to forty-five minutes is a big exception in their lives.

6. Community is something most of them desire, and therefore the lobby, narthex, and gathering spaces are as important as the sanctuary space.

7. They expect to be kept updated through online sources. Anything paper is really strange to most of them if communication could have been handled digitally.

8. They want to give input into just about everything; that is often how they go deeper and engage with things.

9. Most have a network, which is the most important set of relationships in their lives, with the exception of families (although they are digitally connected there also).

10. Meetings and collaborations that can happen virtually are much more convenient than driving to a specific place.

Welcoming

When a new person does decide to physically come to your church, regardless of his or her age, there are common needs they are often experiencing. As we discussed before this, you can assume they have at least mixed emotions, if not a backpack full of negative impressions, when they drive into your parking lot. This is why the welcoming system is so important, because the first impression can never be taken back. Given the speed of life for everyone today, they will usually not give you a second chance to experience entering your church. The churches that are succeeding at attracting and keeping younger people are fully aware of this; in fact, most now have a First Impressions team, which is tasked with everything from the second someone comes onto campus until the second they drive out of the parking lot after their worship experience.

Think in terms of being at a great hotel. People greet you at the front with a "guest services" mentality. Many of these churches have actually used handbooks and principles from these hotels or conference facilities to understand how to treat a guest well when they enter their properties. Why is this so important? Everything for outsiders is unfamiliar—our language, our habits, our way of being together. They will feel much more comfortable if people are attentive to making them feel safe, accepted, and welcomed.

Let's look at the two biblical texts I quoted at the beginning of this chapter from this perspective. The very familiar Zacchaeus story is about Jesus choosing to have dinner with the person everyone hated and would have categorized as one of the "chiefs of all sinners" in their town. Jesus cuts through all of that and indicates he will have dinner with him, which is a relational and accepting gesture, before Zacchaeus had any chance to do anything that indicated repentance, change, or even remorse. No wonder he was freed up to let go of what he had been holding on to so tightly!

That is exactly what guests are feeling when they enter your building and need that hospitable and loving atmosphere to begin to relax about being in church. Many churches have told me that they are very friendly, but usually that is because they now have deep and lasting relationships that are grounded in many years of connection. The newcomers do not have any of that, and the question "Do I belong?" is central to their mind.

It usually is not because people are harsh; it is usually that in their normal routines they don't even see the newcomers in their midst. Typically, interactions with newcomers should not be smothering (the opposite problem), but allow people to engage with some level of comfort and safety. In welcoming churches, this takes many forms, like parking lot attendants, greeters giving direction, visitors' booths to help guide people, screens and signage that direct them to the right places, etc. It can involve welcome letters that are for newcomers, or simply people noticing that they are there. The churches that are making the worship experience outsider-focused are using a lot of resources on what happens in the whole experience of first impressions.

Celebrating

What about the worship services themselves, which I call the celebration system in the church? Most people assume that putting screens in place is the most important change in the sanctuary, but that only touches the surface of what is going on. This is where Paul's principle of becoming like the Romans to win the Romans, or the Greeks to win the Greeks, should be applied inside of churches. What that means, typically, is the worship space team is actually thinking about the whole experience in the worship center, and not just the music or liturgy. The big idea is to make it comfortable and inviting to outsiders, and not lose them in the first hour together.

One well-known example is Willow Creek Community Church in a suburb of Chicago. They are reaching people who are primarily unchurched in their backgrounds. When you drive up, you are looking at a series of buildings that look like a business complex, not a church. You walk into a lobby, not a narthex. You are handed a program, not a bulletin. You walk into an auditorium, not a sanctuary. You see a stage, not an altar. That setup is not for every church, but you can see how they are thinking about the outsider in each decision they make in the worship space. The reason many people rename their worship services "events" or "experiences" is because many of them are planned in all aspects of what is going to happen during the time in this space.

By the way, these experiences differ widely depending on context. In contrast to Willow Creek in Chicago, I know a church in South Dakota that meets in the fairgrounds where the rodeo takes place for the very same reasons—it is familiar and safe to those attending. I know other situations where traditional sanctuaries are changed each week significantly (lighting, music, lobbies, etc.) to make them relevant to people they are reaching.

A worship service or message in the worship space has to do with everything that happens to you while in that space. The younger generations are more accustomed to multimedia ways of learning, inspiring, connecting, etc. In fact, their brains (like all of us) are adapting to this type of learning system in every other aspect of their lives. It is considered boring for many to have one-way audio communication by one person during this time.

Just in case you are having a hard time with this change, I want you to remember the educational ladder you may have been exposed to long ago. We remember only 5 percent of what we hear, but we remember 10 percent of what we see, 25 percent of what we read, 55 percent of what we discuss, 65 percent of what we help create or experience with others, and 95 percent of what we teach others. These new ways of taking in content and learning are actually much more effective.

Nurturing System

The nurturing system in churches that have outsider-targeted environments is also different. The first noticeable difference, for many congregations, is how seriously they take the lobby or space outside the sanctuary. Again, they want to facilitate relationships as much as possible, and a coffee shop, big gathering space, and places to sit and talk allow this to happen. I know one church that serves smoothies in this space, and a different church in a warm climate has a picnic-like gathering after every worship service when the weather permits. Once again, this facilitates a comfortable atmosphere for relationships.

These churches understand that some people who are coming are "beginners" at church and Christianity. They may have all had their own spiritual journeys but possibly have never connected to any organized religion. When you go to an athletic club, for example, you are going to better yourself, not because you are already where you want to be. The personal trainers start where you are in order to help you toward your goals. Likewise, these churches have a goal to start where people need it; some people may not be involved with faith at all. Visitors may go to a discovery class just for people exploring faith, where they can ask questions or express their concerns with the pastors or staff. They may engage with a small group just to build relationships with other visitors or first-time attenders. They may be told they do not need to give until they feel that is a response they would like to make.

The list goes on, but there is no expectation that faith is already part of their experience in these settings. They want to build pathways for newcomers to explore what Christianity is all about. My new-members classes at a church I served began dividing into "discovery" groups for those just learning about faith, and "connection" groups for those who wanted to engage now because they felt confident about their faith. People have no problem dividing into those different groups, and in fact appreciate being allowed to start at the beginning.

To summarize, outsider targeted churches are very focused on the details of welcoming, celebrating, and nurturing outsiders into involvement in the congregational life. They typically have some good knowledge of who the people in their communities are and have planned accordingly. They have actually studied and understood the outsider audiences to adjust these systems to not scare them away by first impressions and opening experiences. Take a look around your community and you can probably find more than one church that has taken these principles and changed what is happening in these three systems. Many times they are the ones with outsiders and young people in their midst.

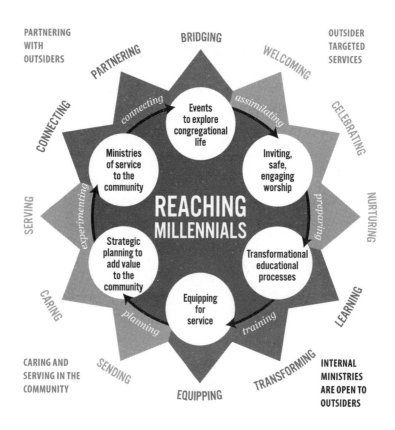

PARTNERING WITH OUTSIDERS

OUTSIDER TARGETED SERVICES

PARTNERING

BRIDGING

WELCOMING

CONNECTING

CELEBRATING

connecting

assimilating

Events to explore congregational life

Ministries of service to the community

Inviting, safe, engaging worship

SERVING

REACHING MILLENNIALS

NURTURING

experimenting

preparing

Strategic planning to add value to the community

Transformational educational processes

Equipping for service

CARING

LEARNING

planning

training

CARING AND SERVING IN THE COMMUNITY

SENDING

EQUIPPING

TRANSFORMING

INTERNAL MINISTRIES ARE OPEN TO OUTSIDERS

CHAPTER 9

Internal Ministries Are Open to Outsiders

They devoted themselves to the apostles' teaching and to fellowship, to the breaking of bread and to prayer. Everyone was filled with awe at the many wonders and signs performed by the apostles. All the believers were together and had everything in common. They sold property and possessions to give to anyone who had need. Every day they continued to meet together in the temple courts. They broke bread in their homes and ate together with glad and sincere hearts, praising God and enjoying the favor of all the people. And the Lord added to their number daily those who were being saved.

Acts 2:42–47

One foundational experience early in my ministry was working part time for Lyman Coleman at Serendipity House in Colorado. Serendipity, back in the 1970s and 1980s, was one of a few centers of small-group ministry in the country. I was in charge of listening to pastors all over the United States and finding out what was working and not working in their congregations. Lyman would always begin his seminar with the text from Acts 2 as the biblical model for Christians to do more than just attend worship services. He would go back to this original vision of living, working, learning, relating, sharing, and being together, and how that lifestyle was so infectious to the people around them that they added to their numbers daily those who were saved.

Fast forward to today, and this reality has become even more important in our digital age. The major reason why is that words have become cheap to us, especially the younger generations, who have been marketed to since they were less than a year old. We touched on this earlier, but Millennials are very sensitive to marketing that is inauthentic; they question the motives behind the people who are delivering the message, questions like the consistency (or lack of) between what someone claims is true and what is really true. Unfortunately, as we learned earlier, 85 percent know and are in relationship with Christians, but only 15 percent see any difference in how Christians live their lives.

I think Rick Warren put well what needs to change for us in the church. He said this in an interview for David Kinnaman's book, *unChristian*: "We need to reconnect the hands and feet to the Body of Christ and be known by what we are for and what we do, rather than just being a big mouth, which is where we are today."[1]

What does all of this mean to us? Churches that are engaging the younger generations know how important it is to connect to outsiders first and foremost in order to simply build trust again in these generations that are skeptical and many times resistant to anything the church does. The learning systems, the transforming systems, and the equipping systems turned toward the community can help break down these walls and build trust. Before we dive into these principles, there is one other thing we need to pay attention to in this whole area—the radically changed society in a digital age.

Digital Society

Over the past forty years, we have witnessed the largest communication revolution in the history of the world. That is not an overstatement. We are still early in this upheaval surrounding information, learning, communication, and community, and the younger generations are the first truly digital generations. It is all so much bigger than websites and video screens because it touches all aspects of life. This change, when rightly understood, is being used to great advantage by many churches.

At Christ Presbyterian Church in the Twin Cities, where I worked during the 1990s and early 2000s, the leadership decided to start new worship services aimed primarily at a GenX audience. It was a completely different worship environment from the Sunday morning experiences, and the young man who was hired to run this new expression of ministry had been a great youth minister for many years before he took on this new challenge. The senior pastor asked me to help this young man interpret the Bible texts that he would be preaching about because he had not been to seminary, and I (while not a Greek or Hebrew scholar at all) was to act as quality control in the situation. We would sit down a couple times a month to look at various texts, and I would bring out the important insights or stories from the passages as we studied them together. For me, messages were typically framed around several points (usually three, in good Presbyterian fashion).

As we worked one afternoon, I asked my young friend what he was thinking about the text as we were considering its importance, because I had already outlined my three points. He shared a wide array of experiences, video clips, witnesses, and physical icons representing a point. I realized that to him, the message was everything that was going to happen to people from the second they walked into the worship center to the second they left. Welcome to a completely new learning world. I did not struggle that long with this change, however, because I had learned a similar lesson in educational forums and small-group environments. I, many times, teach the educational ladder that I mentioned in the previous chapter.

How much do you remember from any presentation?

5% of what you hear

10% of what you see

25% of what you read

55% of what you discuss

65% of what you create with others

95% of what you teach others

Consequently, the brains of the younger generation are shaped by presentations that reach learners on multiple levels. This is reinforced in their experiences in school and has become more and more the norm in their culture. For example, one time I was giving a small-group presentation—something I had given for decades to baby boomer audiences—that included a workbook I provided for people to take notes. At this particular seminar, though, there were two twentysomethings who did not crack the book at all. I was just a few minutes into the presentation when they opened up a dialogue about what I was saying, wanting to contribute feedback to my teaching from their own experience. Welcome to the feedback generation.

Younger people will naturally want to participate, share, amend, etc., the information they interact with. It's part of how they learn in deeper ways. That, by the way, is why much of our traditional teaching processes that are simply one person talking to many, where participants are just listening and taking notes, can seem boring to many in this generation. When you are talking about any learning environment in the church, it is critical that we think participatory, experiential, shareable, and adventurous when possible, as well as fun, multimedia, and interactional.

This just scratches the surface of how the digital revolution is affecting our world. But hopefully it gives you enough background to see how the Learning System, the Transforming System, and the Equipping System can be opened to outsiders. We will take them in that order.

The Learning System

I have written most of this manuscript in a Minneapolis coffee shop called Rustica Bakery. As I was outlining this chapter, two men who frequent this coffee shop were talking with one another about a church event that one of them had attended, apparently part of a luncheon lecture series. I know this church. It is in a downtown setting and regularly hosts lunch lectures to gather many people to hear cutting-edge people speak on various topics, many of who do not attend church. This day was no exception, and the man began to describe what happened. He said that he got there forty-five minutes early and the place was already packed to the gills, standing room only. This is a big sanctuary, so it probably meant a thousand people or more. I thought about how many churches would like to enjoy standing room only in their churches from outsiders attending a luncheon lecture series. What this church did was simply open its learning system to outsiders and put on luncheons that appealed to insiders and outsiders jointly.

As the adult education pastor at Christ Presbyterian Church for twelve years, I had the resources to look at many ways that the education system of the church can be opened to outsiders, and also consulted with many other churches around this area.

Resources were much more limited at a previous church I worked at, a medium-sized one near downtown Denver. As the associate pastor at that church, I was tasked with the growth of the church, inside and outside. Knowing our resource situation, I started with something we were doing well, which was a child enrichment center that took care of latchkey kids before and after school in the neighborhood. Many of the kids were from single-parent families. We were in a time in the church's evolution when most of the people who had joined the church when they lived near the church had physically moved in all four directions around the suburbs of Denver. I knew we had to start trying to attract the people around us again. I thought about all the gifts and talents that various members of our church had in their lives, and I landed on an idea. Since we were already in relationship with single-parent families, I proposed a single-parent family workshop for the adults. I also knew that there was not a very high percentage of churchgoers living around our church. I then decided to hold this workshop in the school across the street because it was safe and already known by many outsiders and was neutral ground.

With this in mind, we printed a flyer that we gave to the kids, and also walked the streets around our church handing them out. I had two psychologists/counselors who were going to run this workshop for six weeks. But I had no idea if this would fly at all.

On the first night I was at the school with the counselors from our church and waited, praying someone would come. On the reputation of the child enrichment center, eighteen adults attended. That was great. After five weeks, I came back to do a little live market research with the group. First, I asked how many of them would have come to this workshop had we put it on at the church. Not a single hand went up. Talk about trust issues. That said, think if you were asked to attend a parent seminar at the mosque or Buddhist temple close to your house. That gives you some idea of what these parents might have felt. I then said we were going to continue the workshop for six more weeks, but the school was charging us to use the facility. I asked how many people would continue to attend the workshop over at the church. Every hand went up. I had to ask, "What happened or what changed in the last six weeks?" One man, speaking for the group, said, "We found out that you people are normal." The group had become open to meeting in the church building only after they trusted the church leaders who were leading them and realized that they and churchgoers have a lot of common ground. That is exactly what is true with Millennials. A top concern is trust. After they experience that, they become open to many more things.

Notice all the principles found in this story.

1. Acknowledge where you are.
2. Understand that the most likely audiences to engage with your ministries are people who have some relational connection already, even if only slightly.
3. Think about what they need or are passionate about.

4. Investigate what talents you already have in the people of the church that might be able to meet that need.
5. Market (hopefully better than we did) and invite people to the learning event you are sponsoring.
6. Make it safe and inclusive as they take this scary step of attending something that a church is sponsoring or hosting.
7. Expect people to trust in stages and do not try to push them too far too fast, but do invite them to go deeper with their relationship to the church.
8. Check in and respond to their feedback every step of the way.
9. Make it at a time that fits their schedule, not yours.

Here are few ideas of how this works in various settings:

- A rural church in Minnesota held a fishing and hunting expo for the area that included workshops taught by church members. While there, many people picked up available literature about other events and ministries at the church.
- In a largely unchurched bedroom community in Washington state, an Alpha Course focusing on marriage is available to everyone. The church building where it is held is packed with people who already give up two hours of their day commuting to and from work.
- A California church writes homeschooling curriculum for anyone in the area who would like to use it. Many families have joined because of its quality.
- A church in Texas puts on men's breakfasts every quarter where an all-male band leads the singing and a well-known guest speaker talks after a member from the church shares his testimony. They have four to five hundred men at every breakfast.

- A Mothers of Teens group gathers for education twice a month to help women in this hard stage of parenting. Many outsiders attend.

Outsiders are hungry for information that will support and better their lives when it really matters to them and they trust you. My family and I have lived in a suburb of Minneapolis for over twenty years, which was most of my boys' childhoods. They attended a school that had many Jewish families, and some of their good friends were from these families. One weekend, I was invited to go on a father-and-son fishing trip with one of these families. Early on in our drive, I asked about Mark's experience with the synagogue and his own background. I was able to share similar experiences in the church, which brought that topic out in the open so it would not stand as a barrier between us. We went multiple years on this trip and had great memories with our sons. On the last year we went, I found out that Mark's wife had had cancer a few years back, but it was in remission. We once again enjoyed the trip, but a short time after we got back, we got a phone call that the cancer had come back with a vengeance, and his wife died within a month. I then had the privilege of going to this Jewish funeral, with many of my younger son's friends, in support of Mark and his family. To my surprise, about a month later Mark showed up at the Mothers of Teens education event. He was now a single dad, and he was not going to let the church/synagogue thing or the male/female thing prevent him from learning what he wanted to know.

The Transforming System (Small Groups, Mentors, Retreats, Spiritual Directors, etc.)

During my growing-up years, we were only marginally involved with the church. So when I went off to college, Christianity was not on my radar. Through a series of God-ordained events, I became a Christian in my sophomore year. I did not even know the names of the Gospels at that point, but I was hungry to learn.

Not knowing anything, I went to an InterVarsity workshop that the leader on campus recommended to me. When I got there, it felt like almost everyone had been a Christian a long time and had been to many such events in their lives. The speaker outlined how to start an evangelistic Bible study in our dorms. Not knowing any differently, I began to do just that in my very secular dorm. I knocked on all the doors and said I was starting a Bible study group, and asked if they would like to come. To my surprise, about eight guys came. We had in the group a Catholic, a Buddhist, a Jewish person, and a couple of Christians who knew I had no idea what I was doing. They asked what we were going to study. We were attending an academically challenging school, so I told them we should study an intellectually tough book of the New Testament. "How about Romans?" I asked. (I had not even looked at the book of Romans, let alone read or studied it.) So we studied Romans.

I shudder at the thought of ever seeing a copy of the videotape of those meetings and what we got out of Romans. But by the sheer grace of God, one of the group members became a Christian. That began my long tenure with small-group ministry. As a leader, pastor, and consultant, I have seen the power of small groups to not only change Christians, but attract and bring many to faith in Christ.

In talking about the small-group system, it is important to understand how differently Millennials think about these environments than the older generations do. To begin with, most Millennials are already living in social networks, with whom their communication is 24/7. When asked how long they are comfortable being disconnected from this world, they will say about an hour. Loyalty to their friends is one of their highest values.

Consequently, they love face-to-face time, but it is much more precious now, and if meetings or questions can be handled through various technologies, it should be (e.g., FaceTime, Facebook, text, tweet, etc.). Millennials want to use their time effectively and efficiently. What that means is support, belonging, feedback, learning, and deciphering are already being handled at least partially for them on the social networks, with which they interact every day.

All of this adds up to Millennials needing a specific purpose for being in a small group. Long-term commitments (open-ended expectations) are not what they desire, at least up front. It's telling that phone companies, like other organizations, are moving away from long-term contracts.

Targeting small groups with interests, needs, and hungers that align with their journeys is important to them. In a similar way, they want to connect to the church relationally. In fact, if young people in youth groups do not build at least one strong friendship with a mentor or friend, they will likely not return to church after college.

There are four major categories of small groups in churches today, with many subcategories.

1. **Task-oriented small groups.** This is when a group (team, board, ministry team, committee) comes together around something they are going to do together.

2. **Relationship-building small groups.** These gather together primarily to build relationships: men's groups, women's groups, fathering teams, professional executive women, etc.

3. **Content-oriented small groups.** These are people who gather to study, learn, and interact with some form of content: livestreams, podcasts, videos, books, curriculums, etc.

4. **Needs-oriented small groups.** In these, people gather together around a common need in their lives, e.g., grief and loss, infertility, job transition.

Let's take a closer look at each of these categories of small groups, specifically at how outsiders can engage with churched people.

Task-Oriented Small Groups

I interviewed leaders of a church in Portland that is one of many churches that are adopting high schools in challenged neighborhoods to make sure all students have basic clothes, backpacks, and school supplies. In this particular church, a team of people is working on preparing all the components that each child will receive in a warehouse area near the church. To their surprise, outsiders began joining their teams to pack these backpacks and help in meeting this need. Millennials, like the generations before them, still have a strong percentage of people who are motivated to make a difference and give back, and doing something rather than just talking about it is right up their alley. A few principles I have seen repeated in these task-oriented groups are:

1. Invite outsiders onto task-oriented teams to join with you to accomplish tasks together.
2. Let the relationships deepen and the Holy Spirit help build a bond of trust.
3. It is best to thank people and celebrate what they do well (think long term here). This is usually the only gateway to hearing about the pains, spiritual lives, or longings they have in their (and our) thirsty souls.

Relationship-Building Small Groups

One of the relationship-building small groups that was popular at Christ Presbyterian Church was the fathering team. Like it sounds, this involved fathers (common interests or need) who gathered together to hold each other accountable to being good fathers and good husbands. Many dads in our setting came to church because their wives insisted that they go and not because they were Christians.

One man, who I will call Carl, came begrudgingly to the team because his wife told him that as a busy surgeon, he likely would barely know his kids unless he was held accountable. As God would have it, Carl ended up in my subgroup of four men within the larger team of twenty-five. In this particular curriculum, we were using the Scriptures about the heavenly Father, which modeled behavior that we should emulate as dads. As we were digesting Scripture week after week, Carl's story came pouring out. He had grown up in Colorado outside the church, just like I had. His father was basically absent from his life, yet was a churchgoer. Carl had a big chip on his shoulder about the hypocrisy of his father attending a church but not even attempting to model love toward his son. Carl had a huge barrier to Christianity because of this experience, and many intellectual questions that needed to be answered before he would even look at Christianity as a faith he would embrace. He was extremely intelligent, and peppered me for weeks with hard questions, which I struggled to help address the best I could. Over the next couple of years, Carl was able to tear down the walls to God and became a man of faith and the co-leader of the fathering team.

A few principles surface from this story:

1. Many people, particularly Millennials, have bad impressions and have had bad experiences with Christians and churches.
2. Many times, outsiders need an opportunity in small-group settings to express their hurt and get it out in the open in front of Christians in order to let it go.

3. The possibility of faith usually is accompanied by many questions, which we need to simply address or even say "I don't know" rather than giving pat answers.
4. At the end of the day, God is the one in these types of atmospheres who brings people to faith.

Content-Oriented Small Groups

One of my favorite stories about the power of content-oriented small groups also happened while I was the new-members pastor at Christ Presbyterian. A couple that was joining the church came to see me for an interview. The husband, whom I will call Jay, said his wife was a Christian but he was not, and that he would like to become one. I immediately began to share the gospel with him, but I noticed him fidgeting. I paused and asked him if this was interesting to him. He said, "Yes, definitely, but I am not ready for all of this yet." I said, "Great. What would help you feel like you belong at Christ Presbyterian?" His answer was surprising: "I want to start a Bible study downtown with my friends." I made an agreement that we would do just that, and I had him invite his friends to the Bible study, many of whom were Christians who had been praying for Jay. You can imagine the phone call from Jay asking his Christian friends to join a Bible study he was starting with me. It was in the context of this small group that Jay's faith began.

Needs-Oriented Small Groups

My wife is a chaplain and a very good facilitator of needs-oriented small groups. She was running a grief and loss small group at our church, and when the week came to speak about forgiveness, she brought me in as the guest teacher. After my talk, two women from outside the church came up to me to get information about joining the church. I was the new-members pastor, but their inquiry to explore membership was so out of context that I inquired why they wanted to do that. (Whoops.) They said they had experienced a level of love in this group that they had never experienced before, and they wanted to know where it came from. Step by step, outsiders were softened by the love of God in this small-group context.

Equipping System

For years I taught a course on leadership at a college in Minneapolis. My students primarily were pastors who worked in poorer neighborhoods among very diverse ethnicities and urban church settings. We had a lot of fun and experienced transformation in our lives as we developed strategies for such a wide variety of settings.

I learned a lot from these pastors, especially how many of them were equipping people around them not just for church ministry but for life. They taught their people leadership, management, and skills training of all kinds. It was from them that I first observed using an equipping ministry to engage with outsiders.

Fortunately, Millennials are very open to mentoring and equipping if it will help them reach their goals. There is a big opportunity here if we expand our thinking to invite and think about what people around us need to improve their lives, and bring more satisfaction and joy.

In my own ministry, two other authors and I banded together to write LifeKeys books, workbooks, and training manuals. LifeKeys help you identify your natural talents, spiritual gifts, personality types, passions, and values in a short period of time. As we began to give this away by training trainers, we were pleasantly surprised that many organizations way beyond the church picked it up and used the LifeKeys tools: life and career coaches, schools and universities, businesses, and nonprofit organizations. More than a few times when I would do a LifeKeys workshop outside the church, the outsiders were just as hungry to learn as Christians.

We saw three motivations beyond God's call on their lives: self-discovery, transitional guidance and direction, and beginning again after hurtful experiences. People enjoyed being with others because this was applicable to their lives, and many became Christians because of this gateway.

A good friend first came to our church through LifeKeys because of a terrible end to a marriage and because she did not like her teaching job. She experienced a lot through that seminar, but by far the most important was a growing openness to faith. She became a Christian and shifted gears to use her teaching gifts in our children's ministry. She then was called to a few other churches, and has been the director of children's ministries for decades now.

Doing this ministry for many years has taught me these transferable principles when you are opening the equipping ministry to outsiders:

1. Many equipping resources and opportunities are online, but if it is important in their lives, people will come.
2. They need to be acknowledged and welcomed even though they do not come from a Christian perspective.
3. Inform them that they are free to share their own perspectives.
4. Make the spiritual input relevant to their lives in the world, not only for inside church work.
5. Do not assume they will believe the Bible has authority just because we claim it does.
6. Once again, let the Holy Spirit do the work of softening their hearts and opening their minds to the gospel.

In a completely different setting, in urban St. Paul, a church was located right next to an elementary school. The senior pastor had a great relationship with the principal of the school. One of the great talents on the school's staff was an Argentinian worship director who had specialized in working with children during his years in South America. He was now doing this at the church each year at both Christmas and Easter, and some of the students began to ask if they could sing with them. When our strategy team heard this, we concluded this was a golden opportunity. The principal, during a school assembly, let the music director motivate the kids to practice and be involved in these shows. Twenty to thirty showed up. As part of that process, we decided to have the dress rehearsal at the school so all the parents could watch their kids in a more neutral environment. Of course they also wanted to see their kids in the real shows that took place in the sanctuary of the church, which were packed for all performances with many families from the neighborhood. That's when the young couples began showing up over time, and they are a big part of the church membership today.

A few principles came out of this experience:

1. Relationships that your congregation and the staff already have with outsiders are many times critical to helping build bridges or clearing the way for engagement.

2. Churches have capabilities they have never thought of, i.e., turning toward the outside or engaging with people outside the church.

3. Let people have a chance to take step-by-step processes to the church. For example, first kids volunteer for an event, then parents are invited to the safe place at the school, then they are welcomed on performance day at the church.

4. Outsiders, in general, actually like to involve themselves with Christians in what they are already doing, rather

than responding to programs designed only for them. It is more like eavesdropping than marketing.

In one youth group, the leader and the junior high director took seriously the development of students in their clubs. These directors would interview potential leaders for various parts of the ministry each year before they were trained to be leaders in the group. But the junior- and senior-high leaders did not leave it there. Each younger student was assigned an older student mentor: seniors with freshmen, juniors with eighth graders, and sophomores with seventh graders. Throughout the year, these older student mentors kept pouring their lives into the students they were engaged with. Needless to say, these became very strong youth groups; many did not leave the church even in senior high. Adult volunteers were mentoring the senior high students as well so they would be more prepared for the world. What actually ended up happening is many kids outside the church joined these youth groups, and through the mentoring processes became developed believers over a period of years. It was like a continuous cycle of training and equipping for the next generation of Christians.

What I learned from interviewing these leaders:

1. We need to constantly equip more leaders to keep bringing new people into a development mode.
2. Together, training and mentoring do a much better job of developing the spiritual lives of people than either would alone.
3. Like Jim Collins said in his book *Good to Great*, it takes a while to get a solid system moving, but once it does, the flywheel has a momentum of its own.

CHAPTER 10

Caring and Serving in the Community

Jesus knew that the Father had put all things under his power, and that he had come from God and was returning to God; so he got up from the meal, took off his outer clothing, and wrapped a towel around his waist. After that, he poured water into a basin and began to wash his disciples' feet, drying them with the towel that was wrapped around him.

He came to Simon Peter, who said to him, "Lord, are you going to wash my feet?"

Jesus replied, "You do not realize now what I am doing, but later you will understand."

"No," said Peter, "you shall never wash my feet."

Jesus answered, "Unless I wash you, you have no part with me."

"Then, Lord," Simon Peter replied, "not just my feet but my hands and my head as well!"

Jesus answered, "Those who have had a bath need only to wash their feet; their whole body is clean. And you are clean, though not every one of you." For he knew who was going to betray him. . . .

When he had finished washing their feet, he put on his clothes and returned to his place. "Do you understand what I have done for you?" he asked them. "You call me 'Teacher' and 'Lord,' and rightly so, for that is what I am. Now that I, your Lord and Teacher, have washed your feet, you also should wash one another's feet. I have set you an example that you should do as I have done for you. Very truly I tell you, no servant is greater than his master, nor is a messenger greater than the one who sent him. Now that you know these things, you will be blessed if you do them.

John 13:3–17

As I was traveling nationally and talking to churches about the themes of this book, one pattern came up consistently. Pastors shared numerous stories about a strong trend amongst the younger generations that often went unnoticed (or perhaps they just didn't know what they were seeing). Namely, young people want to serve in tangible ways, whether locally, nationally, or even globally.

Yesterday I was discussing this encouraging trend with a successful pastor in Minneapolis, and after he thought about it for a moment, he commented, "I was having a talk with a visitor last week who is in his twenties, and he told me the reason he was attending our church was because of our service in the community." The CEO of Feed My Starving Children, currently the largest volunteer organization in the United States, told me that 30 to 40 percent of their volunteers, at various sites, were Millennials. I also brought up this topic with a pastor in the Pacific Northwest whose church gives away backpacks full of school supplies to underprivileged kids. He responded, "Now that you mention it, we do have outsiders come and spontaneously help with this process." There is a service revolution happening in our culture today with the younger generations that provides a great bridge to outsiders around us.

I mentioned earlier David Burstein's wonderful book *Fast Future: How the Millennial Generation Is Shaping Our World*. He shares five perspectives from Millennials that are applicable here:

1. The formative years of Millennials have taught them that resilience and adaptability are essential for survival. The 9/11 attacks, school shootings, etc., took place at key moments in their psychological and intellectual development. The events shaped their worldview, making them more focused on trying to solve the big challenges to come.[1]

2. "Because Millennials have grown up in the fast future, we think of the world practically and pragmatically. We know it as constantly changing and changeable. The problems we face seem bigger and more global. . . . We know we'll be working on solutions to these problems for our whole lives, and we also know we need to get started now."[2]

3. From rock music to sports, young, talented stars have defined those cultural worlds for the last half-century. "Today, however, even ordinary young people who are 'merely' smart, passionate, and engaged with the world around them—not necessarily prodigies—can become standouts by doing amazing things. . . . In previous eras, young people haven't had the resources or tools to bring their ideas and vision into the world instantaneously."[3]

4. "Ordinary people, concerned by a problem, an issue, or an injustice, have been empowered to become extraordinary champions of change. This is the Millennial approach to activism, as well as to business, personal attitudes, and sometimes overall life choices. . . . Millennials have high ideals. But they also know their ideals must be actionable and realizable."[4]

5. "Today's Millennials generally view change in society as a project to work on, not something to demand. . . . Pragmatic idealists are at the center of many of today's youth-led movements, and their thinking and life experiences are very different from those of the radicals who dominated the movement of social change in the 1960s."[5]

All this adds up to a generation of people who want to make a difference, will serve consistently in tangible ways, and derive a lot of satisfaction by rolling up their sleeves. Look around your community and you will see fund-raising walks, runs, and other activities for causes that need help, and often these are organized by younger generations. One reason TOMS shoes is so popular with this generation is because for every pair of shoes you buy, one pair of shoes is donated to a person in need.

Opportunities to give and make a difference are gigantic for the church and for this generation. This is a very attractive part of programming that will be the tipping point of younger generations joining one congregation over another.

Of course, service and serving was a central message of Jesus, perhaps best represented in John 13. By washing his disciples' feet, Jesus demonstrated we are to serve one another. If you want to be great in heaven, he said on different occasions, become a servant of all. He also said his mission was not to be served, but to serve. Paul, the apostle, many times called himself a servant of Christ.

What is unique today is the responsiveness the younger generations have to churches that do serve. In the southwest quadrant of the diagram, there are three ways churches are taking advantage of this to attract outsiders to their congregations: sending, caring, and serving in the community. We will take these one at a time. But first, let me share a story that illustrates the power of this servant movement among Americans today.

One of the greatest positive impacts the American church has had on this nation recently was our response to Hurricane Katrina. Although sometimes not as well organized as it could have been, a great number of people in the South know that long after the government stopped doing anything, groups of Christians kept coming down to help in any way they could.

A pastor in Iowa who I worked with said that sending team after team to clean up the affected areas not only energized his congregation, it became an onramp for young outsiders. They heard what the church was doing and asked to help even before the church reached out for volunteers.

A friend of mine also shared a fun story that paints the picture well. On a return flight to Minneapolis, he sat next to a couple that was dressed as if they were part of a motorcycle gang. My friend struck up a conversation and they all got to know each other. The man and woman were not churchgoers, but they seemed genuinely interested in this church pastor. He thanked them for the good conversation and did not think more about it. The next Sunday the couple from the plane was in his congregation for worship.

One week later they met with my friend for coffee to ask him a question. As the conversation progressed, they revealed that they were independently wealthy and did not need to work for a living. They wanted to ask if my friend would send them out as missionaries to help the world. "We do not know about the God stuff, but we do want to go help where we are needed in the world," they said.

This is the desire the younger generations have to impact their world.

Sending

Sending missionaries out to do God's work is not new for churches. The larger churches usually divide this into local, national, and international missions. This can range from simply financial support for missionaries all the way to large-scale involvement in national and local ministries to their communities. What is changing, however, is who the target audience is that the church chooses to serve with the sending ministry.

The great thing that most churches have in their ministry efforts is their response to the disenfranchised of all types—the poor, the sick, the marginalized, the hungry, the abused, the imprisoned, and others. This is a God-ordained thing, in my opinion, and I strongly resonate with the disciples' emphasis to "remember the poor." But one weakness of this approach is that a church may be serving people across town, in a different suburb, in another state or city, or people overseas, but almost none of their service is to people who would actually consider joining their church or be attracted to Jesus through the congregation's ministries.

When you look at the Gospels closely, Jesus and the disciples often combined service with proclamation or evangelism. In the case of Jesus' miracles, they were meant to be a veritable tractor beam to who he was. Churches that are seeing attendance growth almost always have one aspect of service in the community that impacts people who could turn around and consider engaging with the congregation that has served them.

One great example in Minneapolis is a church that serves free food in the summer, barbecue style, in the parks. Young people walk around offering food to other young people, and then talk about the church they come from, including the many small groups and activities people can try out. What is great about this is it gives people a chance to engage authentically right up front simply by offering food, and they have seen significant growth simply by doing this.

I was working with one church that was across the street from baseball fields that were packed with parents and kids every day of the summer. Because there was not a concession stand, I suggested that we hand out cold water bottles with the church logo to the parents, who probably brought refreshments for their kids but not themselves. The first time we went out, the church volunteers huddled close to the tank of iced bottles of water. I knew we needed to be more proactive, so I grabbed a water bottle and approached a couple. They were reticent at first, but I explained that we were from a nearby church and were simply trying to reconnect with the community, and asked if they wanted water. Soon, the whole team was handing out water, the coaches and refs were asking for water, and word had spread to hundreds of people about what we were doing. Even with this small gesture, we had a woman attend the church the very next weekend. I share this story because the free water was a very simple thing to do, but when we serve people, even in small ways, we are representing Christ's love.

This type of work can ramp up to huge ministries. Churches influenced by Andy Stanley's church in Atlanta have "adopted" nonprofit organizations in their area simply to give them volunteers and resources to succeed. This has a positive effect on how people view the church in the community.

In San Francisco, seventy churches have teamed up to provide social services to the surrounding area. They even have a building close to the government building to house the volunteers and meet a lot of the basic needs of people who are disenfranchised in various ways. Government officials aren't enamored by the churches because of their faith, but they cannot deny that it is the Christians who are rolling up their sleeves and making a difference.

Wayne Cordeiro, a visionary pastor and church planter in Hawaii, told a story that gets to the core of a fundamental shift needed in the church. To a crowd of about four thousand, he announced, "I want to know how many full-time ministers we have." A few hundred hands went up. He thanked them, but then shared how he thought God's plan was to take a full-time minister and disguise him as a teacher so he could influence all the children coming through his classroom. He talked about God taking a full-time minister and disguising her as a software engineer to impact the whole digital space, and taking a full-time minister and disguising him as a stay-at-home dad to be a presence in the neighborhood. Cordeiro added a few more examples, even though his point was clear. "How many full-time ministers do we have in the room now?" Four thousand hands went up. "This is the church of Jesus Christ," he concluded.

The call to be part of the restoration and redemption of God's kingdom extends to each of us. Sometimes, though, this realization takes place only when a person goes on a short-term missions trip. Their full focus is on being on mission for God during the trip. When they get home, it dawns on them that they already are on a mission right where they are.

Caring System

The systems to reach Millennials are all closely interconnected, but caring ministries can be a loving bridge to outsiders of all ages.

I was a part of a church that created what they called a lay care institute. The pastor who ran this ministry helped people in every kind of situation, and equipped a team of people to do the same. Support groups of all kinds were formed and open to outsiders, and the lay care ministers helped in many different ways. One powerful ministry was visiting hospitals to pray with the friends, neighbors, and relatives of church members. It was usually a welcome surprise for patients that a person they didn't even know would come and be with them and pray for them. Through that lay care ministry, we heard many stories of God doing miraculous things and care recipients coming to follow Jesus.

I know of a great story related to the Luis Palau Association in Portland, Oregon, all sparked by a lay person who saw a need and cared enough to do something about it. It all started when a foster mom was visiting the local child welfare office. She saw kids waiting around while social workers found them emergency foster homes. Most of the children had little more than a few items in a plastic garbage bag. The caseworkers tried their best to occupy the children, but the woman was struck by how impersonal and scary the waiting time must be to a child. She asked the officials if she could put together backpacks full of toys and crayons, fun things for kids to do while they were waiting to go to their new homes. The first few backpacks were such a hit that the social workers asked if she could make ten more. Churches across the city got involved and reached out to the community to help. Now "welcome" backpacks and boxes are a standard part of foster home placements in the Portland area.

Care ministries can have a huge impact on a community. They show that Christians care for others, and they provide a tangible bridge to engagement with the church. It is one reason for the many random acts of kindness by churches, Christian radio stations, and others. The old adage continues to be true—I don't care how much you know until I know how much you care.

Serving System

Attracting outsiders through a system of serving has always been close to my heart. When I was preparing for ministry, I was an intern under Bruce Larson at University Presbyterian Church in Seattle, Washington. We tried a program called Love Seattle, and asked the lay people how they would like to serve Seattle in tangible ways. My job as an intern was simply to help people actually accomplish this—no matter how small or big the service.

We had both extremes. I remember one woman in her seventies who told me her world was her apartment complex—"How could I possibly serve Seattle?" she asked. When I found out she had been a professional baker, I asked if her skill could somehow serve the people around her. She came up with a great idea. A number of neighbor kids were by themselves after school until their parents came home from work. It apparently created a lot of chaos and mischief in the complex. She decided to bake cookies so the kids would have something to look forward to. Like the Pied Piper of Hamelin, thirty to forty kids would come to her apartment every day, and she became the surrogate grandmother to a whole congregation of kids.

We also had a man who knew how difficult it was for homeless people to find shelter at night. Computer technology wasn't very advanced back then, so he took it on himself to write software that linked all the homeless shelters in the city so people could look where there were openings and register online.

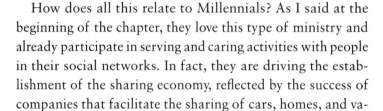

How does all this relate to Millennials? As I said at the beginning of the chapter, they love this type of ministry and already participate in serving and caring activities with people in their social networks. In fact, they are driving the establishment of the sharing economy, reflected by the success of companies that facilitate the sharing of cars, homes, and vacation spots.

I had the privilege to be on the founding board of directors of The Table Project, a social network for churches that connects Christians with each other on a church level, small-group level, and individual level. This organization has developed two powerful apps on their platform (and they are adding more all the time). The first is a prayer app. Anyone on the network can upload a prayer request, and anyone on the network can pray for them and communicate back to the person that they have been prayed for. It is an amazing thing to watch when someone posts a request, and in fifteen minutes a bunch of people have already prayed for them. The other great app is a serve app, which allows people to post when they need someone to help them or serve in some way. People are able to help each other directly without going through church staff or some other process.

As we have discussed, the younger generations naturally support each other in their own networks, both out of necessity and motivation. Whenever I see this it reminds me of Acts 2:44–46: "All the believers were together and had everything in common. They sold property and possessions to give to anyone who had need. Every day they continued to meet together in the temple courts. They broke bread in their homes and ate together with glad and sincere hearts."

I am also reminded of a famous quote credited to St. Francis of Assisi: "We need to preach the gospel to the whole world, and if we have to use words we will." (He may or may not have said this, but it's a valuable insight nonetheless.) Jesus himself wants us to do good works in the presence of outsiders, as taught in the lampstand parable: We are to let our light shine, and the outsiders will see our good deeds and glorify God in heaven (Mark 4:21–23). I also appreciate what French philosopher Simone Weil wrote: "Evangelism is the intersection of everything Christian with everything that isn't." In our day and age, this has never been truer as a way to build trust and tear down negative stereotypes.

Outsiders want to see the kingdom and gospel in action before they discuss the words and truth claims of Jesus. Let us follow Jesus' lead and what he expressed just after washing his disciples' feet: "A new command I give you: Love one another. As I have loved you, so you must love one another. By this everyone will know that you are my disciples, if you love one another" (John 13:34–35).

To many, loving one another *is* a new commandment because that has not been their experience with Christians. Love has and will always be the greatest of things.

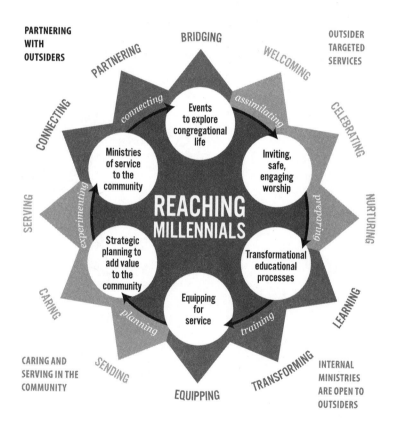

CHAPTER 11

Partnering With Outsiders

"Teacher," said John, "we saw someone driving out demons in your name and we told him to stop, because he was not one of us."

"Do not stop him," Jesus said. "For no one who does a miracle in my name can in the next moment say anything bad about me, for whoever is not against us is for us. Truly I tell you, anyone who gives you a cup of water in my name because you belong to the Messiah will certainly not lose their reward."

Mark 9:38–41

We are in an era of populism today. Crowdsourcing is everywhere. People are being empowered like never before, and the digital-native generations are stepping up and joining forces. In the business world, companies are turning to a talent ecosystem outside their organizations for research, development, and innovation, as well as sales, marketing, and customer service. Institutions of all types are realizing the benefits of group brainstorms and projects.

Millennials have grown up with this connectivity and group decision-making from an early age. I remember watching my sons use instant messaging to communicate with a group of friends simultaneously to figure out what they were going to do that night. Input and participation create buy-in in these generations. This reality creates an enormous opportunity for partnering with outsiders in the networks of your own people and in the communities around your church.

This partnering quadrant on the circle has quite a bit of overlap with the caring/service quadrant, but with one big difference. A partnering relationship with outsiders in our community can go even further in building trust and openness to the gospel. When we partner on things both the church and the community value (think general revelation categories here), we create experiences together that can break down walls, both for us and for them. The backpack of negativity they have toward us (and maybe us toward them) gets unloaded and real relationships can begin. This is happening in so many different ways nationally, but I want to start by grounding this in Scripture.

In my experience, I have not seen Mark 9:38–41 emphasized much in church circles, but I think it shows Jesus' openness to what we're talking about here. The disciples came up to Jesus with a dilemma, though it was framed more as a report than a question. They said someone was casting out demons in his name, so they told the person to stop because he was not a follower of Jesus yet ("not one of us"). The disciples were acting so human here. We all tend to take an "us" and "them" mentality into the world, helping us define what we are and what the "other" is, no matter the issue. Jesus surprises them, however, by saying:

1. Don't stop the person.
2. After someone does a miracle in Jesus' name, they will find themselves unable to speak negatively about it.
3. Whoever is not against us is for us.
4. Even if a person does something as simple as give you a glass of water because you are a follower of Jesus, they will be rewarded.

In other words, the disciples were told that doing Jesus-like acts opens people up to a positive view of Jesus. And if people are not saying they are against you, assume they are for you.

More than ever I find that today's younger generations want to participate in the "stuff" of the kingdom, even if they do not know Jesus. And even more encouraging, the way they buy into the validity of many things is through personal experience.

The reality of this came to me when I first became a Christian on my secular college campus. I lived with a lot of wild guys (drunkenness, inappropriate relationships with women, abuse of drugs, etc.). My roommate was the ringleader. Still, we got along well, and I continued to live out my faith in their midst (which usually meant I saw little of them Thursday nights through Sunday afternoons). One late fall, however, they got in major trouble with the dean of students, who was debating probation for all of them, or even expulsion from school. We had a dorm meeting, and everyone was looking for suggestions on how to improve their reputation with the administration. A crazy idea popped into my head. "We've got a lot of singing, music, and acting talent among us," I told them. "We should put on a Christmas program for the nearby school for mentally challenged students." I was dumbfounded when they all thought it was a great idea.

When we met with the principal to ask about our idea, she looked like she had the weight of the world on her shoulders. She was more than a little skeptical about our plans. Even so, we got the go-ahead and prepared Christmas carols to sing and small presents for the students. We even put together a Santa Claus outfit. The program turned out to be a huge success, and the school was the scene of lots of hugs, presents, and songs. My Christmas present that year was seeing tears flow down the principal's face as we said good-bye and returned to campus.

I was shocked even more by how the guys in my dorm responded. They were clearly excited and deeply moved by what had happened. It was obvious to me that the Holy Spirit had shown up; I know the program opened their lives to the power of God's kingdom.

Connecting, Partnering, and Attracting

At one church, we made a concerted effort to get the whole community involved in a three-day Feed My Starving Children meal-packing event. We publicized it in the local newspaper, contacted Boy Scout and Girl Scout troops, and even reached out to the minimum-security prison nearby. (You can imagine asking the person working on your packing team, "So what are you 'in' for?") We had about eight hundred volunteers, and half were from outside the church. Everyone got a flyer inviting them to celebrate the event in the second worship service that Sunday. The meal-packing event was no bait and switch—we didn't "spring" a worship service on them after their shifts, which is very important for authenticity's sake. People had the choice to come back to the church.

Sunday morning came, and the senior pastor estimated seeing three- to four-hundred visitors at the service. In fact, that Sunday the church was holding its regularly scheduled pancake breakfast for visitors who wanted to learn about the church. Some thought the celebration event would upstage the breakfast, and that it would not go well. Instead, so many visitors were interested in the church and the pancake breakfast that people had to make multiple grocery-store runs to keep up.

These types of events are happening in many thriving churches across America today, and often involve the younger generations. In your community it may not involve feeding starving children, but there are always other options. Young people want to make their communities better places and serve the less fortunate. We need to "not stop them," as Jesus said in the text, but actually create atmospheres where we can do this together.

Connecting

It is easier and easier for people to connect with each other, not just locally but worldwide. The reality for all churches, as we have talked about, is the necessity to use interconnections to be part of people's daily routines. But of all the people around us, with whom should we be connected?

Sometimes in my consulting practice I do a communication audit to identify the major pathways through which people get information about and engage with a church. A vast majority of outsiders get involved with a church by invitation, so we need to take a closer look at the best candidates for your congregation to reach. They are typically:

1. People who live in the church's proximity (thus zip code maps).
2. Those who are engaged relationally with people in your church—friends, family, social networks such as Facebook, etc.
3. Those who are engaged vocationally with people in your church—work colleagues, team members, clients, customers, vendors, etc.
4. Those who share an affinity with people in your church—running-club members, single moms, etc.

To grow, we need to think about helping our members connect in deeper ways with these audiences in their lives and ask them to join opportunities that they would be excited to attend or participate in with us.

Luther Memorial Church in South St. Paul, Minnesota, has a dedicated group of lay people that wants to see the church renewed for the next generations. Even before I started working with them, they were using their commercial-grade kitchen to host an amazing number of food-related events for the community. We built on this momentum by putting on a wider variety of events, including a fall fashion show to support the local clothing bank, a pumpkin carving contest so families could gather together, and bimonthly breakfasts that drew as many outsiders as churchgoers. One woman at the fashion show told me she wanted to be part of this church because they were trying to help their community.

Once you start to see the assets of your campus, and/or the gifts, talents, and passions of some members of your church, connecting becomes very easy. A central question to consider is, How can we add value to the lives of outsiders? Keeping that idea in your mind and focusing on the audiences mentioned above will lead to new connections and engagement with your church.

Partnering

Another gigantic movement today is around partnerships and collaboration. Interconnectedness is allowing for collaboration in so many ways. In fact, as I mentioned in the previous chapter, one of the fastest growing segments of the economy is the sharing economy (think Airbnb, Uber, etc.), and leading the way on this front are the Millennials.

It is interesting to see how this movement mirrors the early church's reality. In Acts 4:32–35 we read,

> All the believers were one in heart and mind. No one claimed that any of their possessions was their own, but they shared everything they had. With great power the apostles continued to testify to the resurrection of the Lord Jesus. And God's grace was so powerfully at work in them all that there were no needy persons among them. For from time to time those who owned land or houses sold them, brought the money from the sales and put it at the apostles' feet, and it was distributed to anyone who had need.

The sense of sharing and not possessing was built into the experience of the early disciples. Today, it is a great way for the church to help and connect with outsiders. A few examples of partnering with the community will illustrate this system.

Many urban churches have created community gardens, where people can grow fruits and vegetables right beside outsiders who join them. The "foodie" movement is strong among the younger generations; knowing their food is fresh and organically grown is a big magnet for them. I even know ministries that have a huge presence in farmers' markets to build bridges to the communities around them. Others grow food for people in need.

In this same vein, some churches organize huge garage sales that are filled with thousands of good, affordable items ready to be reused. One church gives vouchers and special discounts to those truly in need.

Of course, collaboration can be in joint service like Habitat for Humanity has done for years. We were working as a church on one house, and a bank had brought about a dozen employees to join us on this project. We gathered to pray, and said anyone who would like to could join us. Every one of the bank employees stepped forward to join hands with us. No one forced them or put them in an uncomfortable position, which gave them the freedom to enter in.

One easy bridge for churches is to sponsor their own walks, runs, bike events, etc., to raise funds for a local charity, and ask the community to join them. I was working with a church that had held a run for a couple of years, when we decided to open it up to outsiders in a park near the church. It was such a joy to be there on race day and see record crowds come out for the event. Somehow a flyer or poster ended up on a local college campus, and a small group of runners joined in. They were commenting afterward how cool it was that a church would do this, and that they would be back next year. Wouldn't you like to see Facebook pages lit up with pictures and great affirmation of what the church is doing in sponsoring a race? That kind of publicity is gold among the younger generations.

Partnering with the community on common-ground agendas is a wonderful first step for people to learn to trust your church, and perhaps take a step closer to engagement with you.

Attraction

This entire book has been about attracting Millennials and others to Christianity and engagement with a local congregation. But a few principles are critical as you move outsiders closer to involvement.

1. Give people ways to take a next step at every event you engage them in. Perhaps the greatest frustration I see among churches is holding a special event that many outsiders attend, but no one takes a step toward involvement in the church. They need to have invitations, possibilities, or a call to action that is laid out for them authentically and that they feel no pressure to respond to. If you do not plan the next steps as you plan the first interactions with them, usually that will not translate into their actually getting a step closer to your ministries.

2. The aim of all these various methods of engaging Millennials is to build trust, tear down walls of stereotypes, and start relationships with them. It is in that context that the possibility of taking the next steps will bear much more fruit than anything that is impersonal.

3. Realize that the very asking of people outside your church network to participate is an event in itself. Do not get offended or feel bad if they say no or don't have the time. It opens the possibility to talk about spiritual things with them, and often they do not mind at all being asked, if done in friendly, relational ways. People take many touches before they might take a step toward engaging with you, so be patient.

4. Encourage people in your church to spend time before or after an event with friends or other outside connections that participated in the event. Grab a meal or a cup of coffee together. Remember, the Holy Spirit has had a

chance during the event to work on people's hearts, and they may want to talk about a lot of things on a personal level. That deeper connection is so important to people who have taken a chance to be part of a church happening.

I cannot leave this discussion without making a critical point. God is the one who draws people to faith, and our job is to love and engage them, not draw them. Of course, the first step in doing any of this is prayer. Pray when you start, pray every step of the way, pray the day of the event—you get the picture. We are not going to accomplish anything fruitful for the gospel without God being involved every step of the way. If you have it available, please have a prayer team interceding consistently for this work. God will energize and guide the process, work in the event, and draw the people.

Closing Thoughts

would be remiss if I did not mention my ongoing commitment to working with churches to reach younger generations in their congregations. You can visit the website mentioned in the back to learn more, or email me at dstark@businesskeys.com.

That said, my hope is that you now see the vital connection between the right mindset as well as the specific methodology God leads you to embark upon in your setting, whether that is in a church building or not. One thing I always emphasize with people is the reality that God is a strategic God. If you look at Hebrews 11, the so-called Hall of Fame of Faith, you will see that almost all of the stories of great movements of God in people's lives were accompanied by a strategy that God gave these people: Moses and the staff and the preparation to leave Egypt, David and his ongoing leading in defeating the Philistines, Rahab and her obedient response to tie the scarlet scarf on the window, and so on. It is my prayer that God will use the examples presented in this book as a catalyst for a team of people in your church to start experimenting with engaging outsiders, especially Millennials. Don't give up, and remember that we worship a God who can do far more than we can ask or even imagine. May the glory be God's.

Notes

Introduction

1. Pew Research Center, "America's Changing Religious Landscape," May 12, 2015, http://www.pewforum.org/2015/05/12/americas-changing-religious-landscape/.

Chapter 1: The Question Before the Questions

1. David Kinnaman and Gabe Lyons, *unChristian* (Grand Rapids, MI: Baker Books, 2007), 22.
2. Ibid., 40.
3. Ibid., 23.

Chapter 2: Handling Cultural Issues We Know Are "Not God"

1. Kinnaman, *unChristian*, 46.
2. Philip Yancey, *Vanishing Grace* (Grand Rapids, MI: Zondervan, 2014), 116.

Chapter 3: General Revelation—Finding Community and Common Ground

1. Sherry Turkle, *Alone Together* (New York: Basic Books, 2011), 14.
2. Bill Bishop, *The Big Sort* (New York: Houghton Mifflin, 2008), 5.
3. Ibid.
4. Paul Taylor, *The Next America* (New York: PublicAffairs, 2014), 148.
5. Ibid.
6. Ibid., 148–149.
7. Kinnaman, *unChristian*, 119–121.
8. Ibid., 128.

9. Ibid.
10. Yancey, *Vanishing Grace*, 44.

Chapter 4: Disputable Matters

1. Kinnaman, *unChristian*, 181.
2. Ibid., 180–181.
3. Ibid., 177.
4. Ibid., 26.
5. Greg McKeown, *Essentialism* (New York: Crown, 2014).
6. Thom Rainer and Eric Geiger, *Simple Church* (Nashville: B&H Books, 2011).

Chapter 5: The Law

1. David Kinnaman and Gabe Lyons, "Hypocrisy, Authenticity and the Measure of Sin," http://qideas.org/articles/hypocrisy-authenticity-and-the-measure-of-sin/.
2. Kinnaman, *unChristian*, 121.
3. David Burstein, *Fast Future: How the Millennial Generation Is Shaping Our World* (Boston: Beacon Press, 2013), 25–26.
4. Kinnaman, *unChristian*, 83.

Chapter 6: The Gospel

1. Kinnaman, *unChristian*, 72.
2. Yancey, *Vanishing Grace*, 18.
3. Kinnaman, *unChristian*, 66–67.
4. Dave Bennett, "A study of how adults become Christians, with special reference to the personal involvement of individual Christians" (dissertation submitted to the University of Sheffield at Cliff College as part of an MA degree in Evangelism Studies).

Chapter 9: Internal Ministries Are Open to Outsiders

1. Kinnaman, *unChristian*, 243.

Chapter 10: Caring and Serving in the Community

1. Burstein, *Fast Future*, xvii.
2. Ibid., xviii.
3. Ibid., 3.
4. Ibid., xix.
5. Ibid., 4.

David Stark is president of BusinessKeys International, a consulting practice that serves churches as well as businesses. A former pastor, he has worked with churches for more than twenty years, focusing on strategy, leadership, small-group ministries, and lay empowerment.

For businesses, he specializes in strategy, leadership, and culture issues. David is currently working on *Flatwork*, a business strategy book to be published in early 2017.

His previous publications include *LifeKeys: Discover Who You Are* and *Christ-Based Leadership*. He and his family live in Minneapolis. Learn more at davidstarkcollective.com.

More From David Stark

Discover who you are in this insightful guide to uncovering your talents, spiritual gifts, values, and personality. With engaging stories, inventories, self-tests, and other easy-to-use exercises, *LifeKeys* will help you find deeper meaning in life, consider new opportunities, and develop your usefulness to God.

LifeKeys: Discover Who You Are
(with Jane A. G. Kise and Sandra Krebs Hirsh)

With powerful learning tools, thought-provoking questions, and additional exercises, this workbook, when used with *LifeKeys*, will help you understand who God created you to be and the unique ways you alone can contribute to the world.

LifeKeys Discovery Workbook
(with Jane A. G. Kise and Sandra Krebs Hirsh)

⬨ BETHANYHOUSE

Stay up-to-date on your favorite books and authors with our free e-newsletters. Sign up today at bethanyhouse.com.

Find us on Facebook. facebook.com/BHPnonfiction

Follow us on Twitter. @bethany_house